HOWARD ZINN ON DEMOCRATIC EDUCATION

Series in Critical Narrative
Edited by Donaldo Macedo
University of Massachusetts Boston

Now in print

The Hegemony of English
by Donaldo Macedo, Bessie Dendrinos, and
Panayota Gounari (2003)

Letters from Lexington: Reflections on Propaganda
New Updated Edition
by Noam Chomsky (2004)

Pedogogy of Indignation
by Paulo Freire (2004)

Howard Zinn on Democratic Education
by Howard Zinn with Donaldo Macedo (2005)

Forthcoming in the series

Pedogogy of Dreaming
by Paulo Freire

The Globalization of Racism
edited by Donaldo Macedo and Panayota Gounari

Dear Paulo: Letters from Teachers
by Sonia Nieto

HOWARD ZINN ON DEMOCRATIC EDUCATION

HOWARD ZINN

WITH

DONALDO MACEDO

Paradigm Publishers

Boulder • London

Copyright © 2005 by Paradigm Publishers

Published in the United States by Paradigm Publishers, 3360 Mitchell Lane, Suite C, Boulder, Colorado 80301 USA.

Paradigm Publishers is the trade name of Birkenkamp & Company, LLC, Dean Birkenkamp, President and Publisher.

Library of Congress Cataloging-in-Publication Data

Zinn, Howard, 1922-
Howard Zinn on democratic education / Howard Zinn with Donaldo Macedo.
p. cm.
Includes index.
ISBN 1-59451-054-7 (hardcover : alk. paper) — ISBN 1-59451-055-5 (pbk. : alk. paper)
1. United States—History—Study and teaching. 2. United States—Politics and government—Study and teaching. 3. United States—Social conditions—Study and teaching. 4. Democracy—Study and teaching—United States. 5. Politics and education—United States. 6. Education and state—United States. 7. Zinn, Howard, 1922- I. Macedo, Donaldo P. (Donaldo Pereira), 1950- II. Title.

E175.8.Z56 2004
973.931—dc22

2004021697

Printed and bound in the United States of America on acid-free paper that meets the standards of the American National Standard for Permanence of Paper for Printed Library Materials.

Designed and Typeset by Straight Creek Bookmakers.

10   09   08   07   06   05   04
1   2   3   4   5   6

CONTENTS

I
APPARATUS OF LIES USA: INTRODUCTION

Donaldo Macedo

⭗

> Why is President Bush going to war to bring free-
> dom to Iraq and he is passing laws to take away
> freedom at home?
>
> —Alejandro, nine years old

Howard Zinn on Democratic Education is an attempt to analyze a paradox that schools generally face. That is, while schools are charged with promoting a discourse of democ-racy, they often put structures in place that undermine the substantive democratic principles they claim to teach. As a result, schools are necessarily engaged in a pedagogy of lies that are shaped and supported by the interplay of the media, business interests, and the academic enterprise and, believe it or not, by organized labor as well. How else could one explain the overwhelming support that the Bush adminis-tration received in the United States to launch a fraudulent war on Iraq based on lies and deceptions?

It is shocking that a nine-year-old boy can see clearly through the obvious contradiction contained in the current discourse attempting to legitimize an illegal war on Iraq while the media and most Americans—who, by and large, have received higher levels of education—cannot see, for instance, how the Patriot Act that was overwhelmingly enacted by Congress aggressively undermines the Constitution, limiting guaranteed freedom of association and speech. In the name of "security," most Americans have willingly accepted President Bush's directive for neighbors to spy on neighbors, for citizens to lose protection from racial and ethnic profiling, and for citizens and noncitizens alike to be jailed without being charged with a crime and without the right to legal counsel. In fact, a piece published by Walter Pincus in the *Washington Post* cites "FBI and Justice Department investigators as saying that 'traditional civil liberties may have to be cast aside if they are to extract information about the Sept. 11 attacks and terrorist plans.'"[1]

The American propaganda apparatus systematically pointed to the denial of such constitutional guarantees in condemning the lack of freedom that citizens of totalitarian governments in the eastern bloc had to endure during the cold war years. Interestingly enough, during the height of the cold war, when these same rights were violated by government leaders who were considered our friends—such as Pinochet in Chile, Zamosa in Nicaragua, Marcos in the Philippines, the Shah in Iran, only to mention a few startling examples of human rights violators and brutal and despotic dictators—the doctrinal system effectively imposed the necessary ideological blinders that make it possible to selectively see or not see the obvious contradictions and lies. In Chile, for example, Henry Kissinger's observation that "he saw no reason why a certain country should be allowed to 'go Marxist' merely because 'its people are irresponsible'"[2] was successfully turned into a policy designed to overthrow the democratically elected government of Salvador Allende under the auspices of Edward Korry, the U.S. ambassador to Chile, via "a strategy of destabilization, kidnap and assassination, designed to provoke a military coup"[3] that suspended all civil liberties and killed more than three thousand Chileans. Since Pinochet was *our* thug, platitudes about human rights and democracy that are being used against Iraq today did not apply to him.

On closer analysis, the obvious contradictions and lies in U.S. policy that appear to be incomprehensible at first glance make a lot of sense when you consider the role that schools traditionally have played as indoctrination sites where the higher the level of education received, the greater the inability, according to Noam Chomsky, to understand elementary thoughts that any ten-year-old can understand.[4] For example, over 60 percent of college students believed that there was a link between al Qaeda and Saddam Hussein that provided a justification for the invasion of Iraq even though all kinds of evidence clearly shows that there was never a link between the two. In fact, the commission appointed to investigate the intelligence failure during the 9/11 attack concluded that there was no such linkage and that other countries, such as Pakistan, our current ally, provided more substantial and direct material to support al Qaeda. Even President Bush has had to disavow his earlier pronouncements concerning Saddam Hussein's link with al Qaeda, although he continues to use language manipulation that, on the one hand, moves away from his initial categorical proposition that there was a link between Saddam Hussein and al Qaeda and, on the other, reconstructs an association by proposing, instead of a link, a relationship between Saddam Hussein and al Qaeda: "[T]he reason I keep insisting that there was a relationship between Iraq and Saddam and Al Qaeda [is] because there was a

relationship between Iraq and Al Qaeda."[5] Following Ad-
olph Hitler's belief that "the great masses of people . . .
will more easily fall victims to a big lie than to a small
one,"[6] Vice President Cheney continues to disregard all
the official evidence that there was no connection between
Saddam Hussein and al Qaeda by contending that the
"evidence is overwhelming" of a "relationship."[7]

Against an orchestrated bombardment of lies facilitated
by a pliant media, one can understand, after critical reflection, why these same students and a very high percentage
of Americans continue to blindly accept the administration's initial lie, which is kept alive, periodically, by Vice
President Cheney in his absolute, albeit false, contention
that such linkage exists without providing a shred of evidence to support his claim. If not for a high level of indoctrination, these same students, along with the media and
political pundits, would have to maintain some level of
coherence and apply the same rationale they have used to
justify the bombing, invasion, and occupation of Iraq by
proposing to do the same to Pakistan since, according to
the commission investigating the 9/11 attack, Pakistan
supported al Qaeda for years.

Given the high level of indoctrination students receive
in schools supported by media propaganda reminiscent of
totalitarian socialist states, Howard Zinn states that he is
"not surprised that 60 percent of college students would
think something like the linkage between al Qaeda and
Iraq is absolutely true, because they didn't get anything in
their education that would prepare them to look critically
at what the government says, so they listen to the government say again and again and again that something is true
or hint and suggest and make connections, and then when
the president denies it in one statement, it's not enough to
penetrate what has already become a mountain of lies"

(p. 54, this volume). This mountain of lies is part of the indoctrination process that imposes a willful blindness to evidence and contradictions.

These lies and contradictions are more readily embraced by the educated class to the degree that the more educated and specialized individuals become, the more interest they have invested in the system that provides them with special privileges and rewards. For this reason, we often see people whose consciousness has not been totally atrophied, yet they fail, sometimes willfully, to read reality critically and they often side with hypocrisy. In most cases, these individuals begin to believe the lies, and in their roles as functionaries of the state, they propagate these same lies. That is why, for example, according to Noam Chomsky, the majority of the educated class supported the war in Vietnam while it was being waged, whereas in 1982, according to a Gallup poll, over 70 percent of the general population said the Vietnam War was "fundamentally wrong and immoral, not a mistake."[8] Characterizing the Vietnam War, as well as the atrocities committed by American GIs, as a mistake, as Robert McNamara, one of the architects of the war, has done, removes both responsibility and accountability from those who should be tried by the World Court for their horrendous crimes against humanity.

This represents yet another example that supports the contention that more education does not necessarily entail greater ability to read reality critically and accurately. The indoctrination that students receive in schools is acknowledged by the Trilateral Commission, whose members—among them former President Jimmy Carter—state that schools should be designed "for imposing obedience, for blocking the possibility of independent thought, and they play an institutional role in a system of control and coercion."[9] Given the indoctrinating mission of schools, we should join Howard Zinn's sense of encouragement, optimism, and hope "that *only* 60 percent of college-educated people believe [the allegation of a link between al Qaeda and Saddam Hussein], since from what they get from the educational system, it should be 95 percent" (p. 54).

The "weapons of mass deception" used by the Bush administration to "manufacture consent" for the Iraq War gives credence to Hitler's proposition that the effectiveness of any propaganda machine depends largely on big lies rather than small ones. It does not matter that no weapons of mass destruction were found; neither does it matter that Iraq did not possess "30,000 warheads, 500 tons of chemical weapons, 25,000 liters of anthrax, 38,000 liters of botulinum toxin"[10] as the president claimed in his 2003 State of the Union Address. It does not matter that the illegal war on Iraq has already killed "approximately 11,000 to 15,000 Iraqis," of which "between 3,200 to 4,300 were non-combatant civilians,"[11] nor that, if necessary, we might carry out Sen. Trent Lott's threat that "if we have to . . . we'll just mow the whole place down, see what happens."[12] It does not matter that the war on Iraq has become an international travesty conducted in defiance of "a spectacular display of public morality [when] 10 million people on five continents marched against the war in Iraq."[13] What matters is that President Bush acts like a macho-man John Wayne–light who makes tough decisions and unilaterally dismisses the opinions of 10 million people worldwide because he's tough enough not to base his policies on "focus groups." What matters is that we support our troops while the Bush administration cuts billions of dollars in veteran benefits limiting access to health care and programs designed to aid troops' reentry into civilian life. What matters is that we heed the jingoistic, chest-pounding patriotism of "bring 'em on" while the media become bona fide cheerleaders whipping the citizenry into a war frenzy to exact revenge for the cruel attacks on the World Trade Center that killed more than three thousand people.

As we rightly mourn and denounce the killing of innocent civilians in the World Trade Center, we must also recognize the pain of the families of more than three thousand Iraqis, innocent civilians, who have been the victims of our capricious and destructive missile attacks. These families' pain does not diminish in the language manipulation that reduces the act of mass killing of civilians by our guided missiles to the euphemistic phrase *collateral damage*. Whether it is labeled a terrorist act when carried out by planes turned into missiles or an act of war when carried out by our guided missiles, the terror inflicted on civilians in both instances remains the same. For instance, in May 2003, a U.S. missile struck a wedding party in Iraq, killing forty-five family members. For the relatives who survived this cruel attack, these supposedly guided missiles are part of our fabricated high-tech war in Iraq, which is controlled by ever-increasing technological wizardry, ephemeral sound bites, metaphorical language, and prepackaged ideas void of substance. But rather than being mesmerized with "shock and awe" at the near-precision landing of our "smart bombs" during aseptic "surgical strikes," these Iraqi civilians experienced the same kind of terror that in the United States is symbolized by the box-cutter-wielding terrorists who turned planes into deadly weapons. The jingoism and our need to exact revenge for the 9/11 attacks should not, however, blind us to the shameful fact that, according to Michael Berg, who lost his son in Iraq, "there are 11,000 plus Iraqi citizens that are dead and each one's family is as affected as I was, but the American media doesn't cover these people. It doesn't cover the people who are suffering the most."[14]

The inability to empathize with the sufferings of innocent civilian Iraqis who were also victims of terror gave rise
to a jingoistic, post-9/11 national mourning that required
politicians, the media, and citizens to use the American
flag as blinders, preventing even the most liberal and well
informed to give up the democratic right to question and
instead to blindly support the newly coined proposition of
a "war on terror." As a result, after 9/11 not wrapping
oneself in the flag constituted an unpatriotic act. If one
were to argue that patriotism involves a lot more than a
jingoistic display of waving the flag—that it is more patriotic to work to make the country more democratic, more
just, less racist, and more humane—one would probably
be accused of a lack of patriotism or even of being anti-
American. If one would point to the vulgar commercialism
of the flag after September 11, ranging from American flag
thong underwear to condoms designed in red, white, and
blue, one would also be charged with a lack of patriotism.
If one pushed the envelope further and pointed out that
the leaders of our country were hiding behind the flag to
promote one of the largest shifts of wealth from the poor
to the rich via tax cuts and corporate subsidies ($15 billion
to the airline industry alone) while cutting services to the
poor and elderly and slashing funds for education and social services, including benefits for the very troops that the
administration is asking us to support, the reaction would
again be more finger-pointing about one's lack of patriotism. And if one went so far as to link the undemocratic
nature of U.S. foreign policy with the present worldwide
hatred of the United States, the possibility for further dialogue just might collapse.

During the Iraq War, the American flag has played the
role that the yellow ribbon had played during the first Gulf
War, effectively suffocating any truly democratic dialogue.

During the Gulf War, the yellow ribbon did more to ideologically cage the American mind than all the speeches given by politicians. And after 9/11, the American flag patriotically tied American minds by making them sufficiently complacent so that they would comply with the manufacture of consent for a fabricated and illegal war. The high level of domestication of the mind is evidenced in the total lack of outrage toward the falsehoods that informed and shaped the justification of the Iraq War, ranging from the falsification of documents used by the Secretary of State, Colin Powell, in his justification for war before the Security Council to President Bush's false claims in his State of the Union Address, in which he contended that Iraq possessed weapons of mass destruction. It does not matter that no weapons of mass destruction have been found, because over 66 percent of the population continued to support Bush's policies even when the facts point to the lies and deceptions that undergird these policies. Even when Deputy Secretary of State Paul Wolfowitz, one of the major architects of the war, stated in an interview with *Vanity Fair* that the concern over Iraq's weapons of mass destruction was never a primary reason to go to war but only a bureaucratic decision to unite people for the war, the American people seem to be unbothered by the big lie as they remain wrapped in the American flag, a behavior that provides "otherwise alienated human beings a sense of cohesion . . . [while] purg[ing] unconscious guilt and reinforc[ing] feelings of virtue."[15]

Thus, in order for most Americans to protect the low foundation of their virtues, it becomes imperative that they continue to support the war even though it has now become evident that the reasons given by the administration for the Iraq War were fraudulent. As a consequence, they prefer to remain loyal to the jingoism represented by the

American flag that, in a direct and successful way, structured the Iraq War debate so as to brook no dissent or debate. After 9/11, criticizing Bush administration policies was viewed as anti-American. Questioning Bush's administration after the war began was cleverly manipulated as not supporting our troops. In fact, this is precisely what happened during the media cheerleading of the war preparation, when, for instance, in the U.S. Congress, one would risk losing one's seat if one dared question the president's war policies in Iraq. Given the overwhelming evidence of the Bush administration's mass deception, the media are belatedly attempting to rescue their image of objectivity as evidenced by the recent *New York Times* editorial that stated that "there was never any evidence of a link between Iraq and Al Qaeda, between Saddam Hussein and Sept. 11,"[16] "and demanded an 'apology' to the American people from President Bush."[17] The *New York Times* should also demand that Congress apologize to the American people, since it has become a rubber stamp to ratify all of the policies of the conservative agenda and in which the ideological distinctions between Republicans and Democrats have simply collapsed. In reality, the Democratic Party, in its role as the opposition party, simply became a lapdog for an otherwise belligerent, reactionary, and unprincipled Republican Party. More important, the *New York Times* should demand that both Congress and President Bush apologize to and make financial reparations to the relatives of the eleven thousand Iraqis killed by our illegal war. Moreover, the *New York Times* should also remind the U.S. administration that the rules of law should be applied universally and not unilaterally rather than be applied only to Saddam Hussein, Osama bin Laden, and those the administration characterizes as "enemy combatants." This means that the International Criminal Court in

The Hague should be given jurisdiction to indict President Bush and his commissars for their violation of international laws by waging an illegal war on Iraq and by violating the Geneva Conventions, exemplified in the Abu Ghraib torture of Iraqi prisoners and by the amply documented human rights violations committed by the U.S. military in both Iraq and Afghanistan. It is no wonder that the United States would be vehemently against the existence of the International Criminal Court and has launched an aggressive "diplomatic campaign to compel other countries to sign bilateral agreements exempting U.S. citizens, whether military or civilian, from potential jurisdiction of the new International Criminal Court in The Hague."[18]

Against a backdrop where "it's the defeated who are tried and not the victors,"[19] it is unlikely that President Bush and his commissars will ever face justice in court, and in order to assure the victorious Americans a sense of rectitude and moral high ground, it becomes imperative that history be written from the victors' perspective. This requires that the enemy's story never be told, which means that the teaching of history must be manipulated and distorted through a type of educational training that makes it possible for us to rally behind our political leaders wrapped in the American flag, who ritualistically call for the protection of human rights all over the world, without our recognizing that these same leaders are complicit in the denial of rights to the human beings who live under the cruel dictatorships that we support either overtly or covertly.

The teaching of history from the victors' point of view invariably imposes historical blinders so as to keep the citizenry docile, domesticated, and historically ignorant, even though this ignorance is never innocent. That is, those who are either willingly or unwillingly historically ignorant are still actors of history and, as a result, are ultimately implicated in the making of history. The victors' teaching of history must inevitably rely on a pedagogy of big lies that gives rise to historical amnesia.

Had it not been for historical amnesia, how could we accept Bush's propositions that "states that harbor terrorists are as guilty as the terrorists themselves"[20] and, as a consequence, that the United States has the right to wage war against such states as we did aggressively in Afghanistan? Noam Chomsky correctly argues that if we apply this doctrine universally and not unilaterally (meaning that the doctrine does not apply to the United States), Washington would have to bomb itself, because the harboring and/or training of terrorists on U.S. soil is an integral part of our history. Let's not forget that the United States was a main supporter of terrorist militias in Afghanistan, including militants like Osama bin Laden, that waged war against the Soviet occupation of that country. Had it not been for historical amnesia, we would remember the material and intelligence support that the United States provided Saddam Hussein when he invaded Iran, a war that caused more than one million deaths. When Saddam Hussein was our friend, we showed no displeasure at his use of chemical weapons against Iranians. In fact, the propaganda apparatus was working overtime to keep us from learning about our complicity in the atrocities and carnage of the war between Iraq and Iran.

A simple test unveils our double standard concerning the U.S. posture regarding cruel dictators like Saddam Hussein. For the sake of argument, let's say that during the standoff between President Bush and Saddam Hussein, as Americans were being drummed up for war, an Iraqi warplane had fired a missile at an American frigate, igniting a "huge fire that damaged the frigate heavily"[21] and killing a number of sailors. How would the United States respond to such an unprovoked attack? At the very least, it would have spared President Bush the need to fabricate lies providing a rationale to attack Iraq—lies that included stories of weapons of mass destruction and the categorical belief that Iraq could use these weapons within forty-five minutes, creating an urgency to launch a preemptive attack. The United States would have milked the United Nations, despised by the Bush administration, for all the necessary diplomatic public relations, ensuring world support to counteract Iraq's aggression. The attack would have been brutal and decisive, and there would have been no limit to the power used to destroy a tentacle of the "axis of evil." This unchecked power to wage preemptive war would have also included the use of small nuclear bombs, as was widely discussed by Bush policy makers. Most Americans would have more or less agreed with this response and, certainly, would also have supported what would be viewed as a provoked war.

The events I just described did not happen in 2003, but they did take place during the war between Iran and Iraq, when Iraq was considered a friend and an ally to the United States even though it was ruled by the same cruel and despotic dictator, Saddam Hussein, we attacked in March 2003. In 1987, an Iraqi warplane attacked a U.S. frigate in the Persian Gulf, causing serious casualties. However, the U.S. response was diametrically opposed to what would be expected in 2003. In fact, in 1987, the U.S. media went out on the limb to soften the news. According to a *Boston Globe* report, "A US guided-missile frigate patrolling in the Persian Gulf was attacked by Iraqi aircraft yesterday in what appeared to be an error, the Pentagon said."[22] True to their servitude to the power structure, the media often take their cues from the administration and report accordingly. In this case, the Pentagon saw fit to protect Saddam

Hussein, leading Robert Sims, the Pentagon's chief spokes-man, to state, "We believe this was a mistaken attack. . . . There is no indication of any deliberate, hostile intent."[23]

The question that needs to be raised is why there was no outcry and flag-waving against Iraq then for this unprovoked attack while there was an avalanche of support to attack Iraq in 2003, when there was no evidence that it had acted aggressively against the United States? The answer to this simple question would unveil the lies that usually inform our foreign policies and the present antiterrorist doctrine of the Bush administration is no exception. According to Chomsky, a very short list of examples would suffice to unmask U.S. complicity with the harboring and training of terrorists:

- The U.S. launched a terrorist war against Cuba in 1959. It picked up rapidly under Kennedy, with Operation Mongoose—a major escalation that actually came close to leading to nuclear war. And all through the 1970s, terrorist actions against Cuba were being carried out from U.S. territory, in violation of U.S. law and, of course, international law.

- There is Orlando Bosch, for example, whom the FBI accuses of thirty serious terrorist acts, including participation in the destruction of the Cubana airliner in which seventy-three people were killed back in 1976. The Justice Department wanted him deported. It said he's a threat to the security of the United States. George Bush I, at the request of his son Jeb, gave Bosch a Presidential pardon. He is sitting happy in Miami, and we are harboring a person whom the Justice Department regards as a dangerous terrorist, a threat to the security of the U.S.

- The Venezuelan government is now asking for extraditions of two military officers who were accused of participation in bombing attacks in Caracas and then just fled the country. These military officers participated in a coup which, for a couple days, overthrew the government. The U.S. openly supported the coup and, according to British journalists, was involved in instigating it. The officers are now pleading for political asylum in the U.S.

- Emanuel Constant, whose death squad killed maybe 4,000 to 5,000 Haitians [during the early 1990s while he was on the payroll of the CIA]. Today, he is living happily in Queens because the U.S. refused to even respond to requests from Aristide for extradition.[24]

We could easily add to this list by citing scores of former Latin American military officers trained by the United States who committed all kinds of atrocities against their own people and who are now living tranquilly in the United States. We can also cite the School of the Americas, a notorious institution for training Latin American military officers who have gone on to commit countless crimes against humanity, such as the murder of six Jesuit priests (including the rector of a university), their housekeeper, and the housekeeper's daughter in El Salvador in 1989. The El Salvador military also murdered the Maryknoll sisters (all Americans) in 1980 and was responsible for the assassination of Archbishop Oscar Romero during a mass on March 24, 1980, with the complicity of the U.S. government. The School of the Americas even had a curriculum designed to train military officers in the techniques of torture, assassination, destabilization, and terrorist attacks. All of these activities were fully supported by the U.S. government and our tax dollars, and if the antiterrorist doctrine were to also apply to U.S. officials, they would have to be forcibly sent to Guantánamo without any legal right to counsel as is currently happening to those designated "enemy combatants."

The obvious contradictions described so far point to an intricate and complex web of lies that functions to reproduce the dominant ideology through the interplay of the media, education, and the business sector. This becomes clear if one unmasks, for example, how schools play an important role in cultural reproduction, where collective experiences function in the interest of the dominant ruling elites rather than in the interest of the oppressed groups that are the object of the policies of cultural reproduction. That is why, as Howard Zinn argues, schools never allow a curriculum that "tell[s] the story . . . from the standpoint of the other side, of 'the enemy.' To tell the story of the Mexican War from the standpoint of the Mexicans means to ask: How did they feel about having 40 percent of their territory taken away from them as a result of the war? How did they view the incident that President Polk used as a reason for the beginning of the war? Did it look real or manufactured to them?" (p. 189).

In essence, in teaching history from the standpoint of the enemy, Howard Zinn proposes a pedagogy based on the juxtaposition of historical texts and contexts that will enable students to interlink the flux of information in order to gain a more critical reading of reality. Instead of just domestically consuming historical facts presented in a decontextualized manner, students can rely on other points of reference so that they can be free to think more critically (something that is often discouraged in schools) and recognize the falsehoods embedded in the various pedagogies created by the dominant class. By and large, dominant education utilizes poisonous pedagogical mechanisms to undermine independent thought, a prerequisite for the "manufacture of consent." It is only through a pedagogy that manufactures consent that a society tolerates gross distortions of reality as we are witnessing with the present war in Iraq and the rewriting of history as exemplified in an extract from *The History of the United States,* by Robert J. Fields, used as a social science text in some of the Boston Public Schools.

Vietnam is a small country near China. It is thousands of miles from the United States. Vietnam is on the other "side" of the world. But, it hurts our country badly. . . . The Vietnamese people fought for their freedom. Communists took advantage of the fight. Communists wanted to make Vietnam a communist country. The people of Vietnam just wanted freedom. . . . The North Vietnam army fought a secret war. They hid and ambushed the Americans. Women and children helped fight against Americans. . . . Thousands of American soldiers died in Vietnam. Many Americans were against the war."[25]

What this text clearly demonstrates is how history is distorted not only by the presentation of false historical information but also by the omission of other important historical facts that serve as a counterpoint of reference. For example, in his rewriting of the history of the Vietnam War, Robert J. Fields failed to account for the more than one million Vietnamese people who died in the war, not to mention the systematic killing of the elderly, women, and children by Americans, as evidenced in the My Lai Massacre.

Following Howard Zinn's pedagogical proposal, students would be asked how they would feel about witnessing the mass killing of the elderly, women, and children. According to Zinn, "when students are asked, 'Is this right, is this wrong?' then it becomes interesting, then they can have a debate especially if they learn that there's no simple, absolute, agreed upon, universal answer" (p. 191). By using a nonofficial perspective of history, students studying the Vietnam War would learn that the My Lai Massacre was not an isolated, bizarre incident where a handful of U.S. troops went crazy. Similar massacres were routine, as Sergeant James Daley recalls: "'When you come into the enemy village,' we were told [by training instructors in the United States], 'you come in opening fire. You kill everything that's living—women, children, and animals.'"[26] Given the kind of training that U.S. soldiers receive, it should not be surprising that the current atrocities committed in Iraq represent, "[n]ot just the long and copious documented record of U.S. torture, with many refinements acquired by the CIA from the Nazis after World War II, but the more recent lineage of encouragement."[27]

Sergeant James Daley's account proves that the My Lai Massacre was not an isolated incident. In fact, Shad Meshad, a psychologist who served in Vietnam, described what he had heard from soldiers: "They'd been on sweeps of villages, with orders to leave nothing living, not even chickens and [water] buffaloes. Well, what the fuck did that mean, following orders like that? Wasn't it Lieutenant Calley who created the stir in the first place? They were doing a Calley every day."[28] The soldiers now indicted for torturing Iraq prisoners at Abu Ghraib prison could easily borrow from the script described by Shad Meshad of what he had heard from U.S. soldiers in Vietnam: "Well, what the fuck did that mean, following orders like that?"

Although the vicious acts of violence perpetrated against innocent Vietnamese women and children by our GIs are well-documented facts, one never reads in school history books about U.S. crimes against humanity because history is never taught from the perspective of the enemy. Thus, it is not surprising that cultural commissars like teachers, political pundits, and many journalists choose to selectively monumentalize certain aspects of U.S. history while neglecting to report on heinous crimes that the United States has systematically committed in the name of "freedom" and "democracy." Instead, we create schools designed to reward the so-called good student, "who repeats, who renounces critical thinking, who adjusts to models . . . [who] should do nothing other than receive contents that are impregnated with the ideological character vital to the interests of the sacred order."[29] A good student is the one who piously recites the fossilized slogans contained in the Pledge of Allegiance without understanding the true meaning of the democratic ideals proposed in that pledge. A good student is the one who willfully wraps him- or herself in the flag and unreflectively accepts as given the big lies.

Tom Paxton captures how history is distorted in schools through a pedagogy of lies in his song "What Did You Learn in School Today" when the student tells his parent,

> I learned that Washington never told a lie,
> I learned that soldiers seldom die,
> I learned that everybody's free. . . .[30]

History is distorted in schools through a pedagogy, according to Howard Zinn, in which the teaching of "the history of war is dominated by the story of the battles, and this is a way of diverting attention from the political factors behind a war. It's possible to concentrate upon battles of the Mexican War and to talk just about the triumphant march into Mexico City and not about the relationship of the Mexican War to slavery and to the acquisition of territories that might possibly be slave territories" (p. 189). In the same manner, the future teaching about the Iraq

War will probably be told in terms of the battles, with much celebration of U.S. technological wizardry and the massive firepower of our guided missiles while reducing the killing of more than eleven thousand Iraqis to the gutless euphemism of *collateral damage*. The story that will never be told from the victor's perspective is that the Iraq War was an illegal war, based on fabricated falsehoods, that summarily slaughtered thousands and thousands of innocent civilians, including women and children. If fact, we can count on historians such as Robert J. Fields to rewrite history that will later be taught to students. He might write that "[Iraq] hurt our country badly. . . . [The Iraqi] people fought for their freedom. [Terrorists] took advantage of the fight . . . they hid and ambushed the Americans," substituting Iraq for Vietnam and terrorists for communists.

Fields's history of the Vietnam War remains intact, and good students will recite verbatim the lies told by the teacher. Noam Chomsky suggests that "[n]ot everyone accepts this. But most of us, if we are honest with ourselves, can look back at our own personal history. For those of us who got into good colleges and the professions, did we stand up to that high school teacher who told us some ridiculous lies about American history and say, 'That's a ridiculous lie. You're an idiot.' No. We said, 'All right, I'll keep quiet, and I'll write it in the exam and I'll think, yes, he's an idiot.'"[31]

Howard Zinn on Democratic Education not only debunks the traditional distortions of the teaching of history but also urges all educators to embrace a critical approach to education, where "the issue of class and class conflict needs to be addressed more honestly because it is ignored in traditional nationalist history" (p. 194) where "[t]he complicity of poor white people in racism [and] the complicity of males in sexism" are unveiled (p. 195), and where "[historical] objectivity is neither possible nor desirable. It's not possible because all history is subjective; all history represents a point of view" (p. 198). What is important is that pedagogical opportunities be available for students to learn from dangerous memories so large-scale human atrocities such as the Holocaust are not repeated.

For that to happen, educators, instead of engaging students in a distorted triumphalist national history lesson, need to ask students to look at U.S. history through a magnifying glass so they can see the grotesque and barbaric images of slavery, the Vietnam War, class conflict, gender exploitation, the sabotage of democracy in Latin American countries, and now the illegal war waged against Iraq. An honest account of U.S. history should also include taking students to a museum of slavery, with graphic accounts of the dehumanization of African Americans, where families were split apart and sold on the block to the highest bidder and where pictures of lynching would remind us of our racist fabric. Students should also be taken to a museum of the quasi genocide of the American Indians, their enslavement, and the raping and expropriation of their land. Students should also be encouraged to learn about the Indian Imprisonment Act, which authorized the jailing of American Indians who attempted to enter Boston, their own land. Some students may argue that this law was enacted so long ago that it belongs to the dustbin of history and that our democracy is incapable of committing such blatant discrimination today. Without talking down to students who hold this view, teachers could engage them by juxtaposing the Indian Imprisonment Act with the current U.S.-supported policies of Israel, such as checkpoints designed to keep Palestinians from traveling freely in their own land. The teacher may also share with his or her students the fact that the International Court of Justice at The Hague "ruled . . . that Israel's separation fence contravenes international law, that it must be dismantled, and that compensation must be paid to the Palestinian owners of property confiscated for its construction."[32] Since the International Court of Justice's ruling is nonbinding, it behooves the United Nations Security Council to impose sanctions. Students can then be asked to hypothesize whether the United States would veto the Security Council. Without imposing his or her opinion on students, the teacher could engage them in the analysis of the U.S. veto history in the Security Council to see what pattern would emerge as a means to measure the accuracy of their assumptions concerning the U.S. posture vis-à-vis this recent ruling of the International Court of Justice against Israel. Students would learn for themselves that the United States stands practically alone in the world in support of Israel's occupation and expropriation of Palestinian land. They would also learn about the United States' arrogant dismissal of the World Court rulings, for example, when the World Court ruled against the United States for violating international laws by mining the Nicaraguan harbor, a terrorist act if the definition of the term is applied universally. Students should also be taken to a Vietnam War Museum, along with the Vietnam Memorial, where graphic accounts of the rape and killing of Vietnamese women by U.S. GIs would be described.

The girls were unconscious at that point [after repeated rapes]. When they finished raping them, three of the GIs took hand flares and shoved them in the girls' vaginas. . . . No one to hold them down any longer. The girls were bleeding from their mouths, noses, faces, and vaginas. Then they struck the exterior portion of the flares and they exploded inside the girls. Their stomach started bloating up and then they exploded. The stomachs exploded and their intestines were just hanging out of their bodies.[33]

Students could be asked to juxtapose the texts and contexts where insurgents, for example, in Iraq where they would hypothetically rape American girls in the same manner. They would be asked what the appropriate reaction of the U.S. officials and the public would be. Their response would be one of outrage, and possibly Defense Secretary Donald Rumsfeld would accuse the Iraqis of violating the Geneva Convention as he did when, in the beginning of the Iraq War, some American soldiers were shown on television being questioned by their captors. It is the same Rumsfeld who was quietly, at the same time, approving interrogation methods that violate the Geneva Convention, which were applied first in Afghanistan when he stated that it is "my hope that [the fighters] will be either killed or taken prisioner."[34] These prisoners were held in containers in which, when they were opened, "a mess of urine, blood, feces, vomit and rotting flesh was all that remained."[35] Students would begin to see for themselves that the reported torture in Abu Ghraib is not an aberration or an isolated case of human rights violations committed by some uncaring GIs but a continuation of an official policy that had its prelude in Afghanistan.

By juxtaposing historical texts and contexts whereby various points of reference are taken into account, as Howard Zinn suggests, students, in particular, and the public, in general, will begin to be able to link the necessary bodies of knowledge to develop a more critical and comprehensive understanding of reality. If our education systems don't change, schools will continue to produce highly literate individuals who willfully or unwillfully do not see the obvious, which any nine-year-old would have no difficulty seeing. That is why approximately 60 percent of college students believed President Bush's lies in the present Iraq War and why semiliterate former Vice President Dan Quayle, who can't even spell potato correctly, was able to see the obvious contradictions in his administration's policy toward Iraq when he read the first Gulf War correctly as "a stirring victory for the forces of aggression."[36]

NOTES

1. Alexander Cockburn, "Green Lights for Torture," *The Nation*, May 31, 2004, 9.

2. Christopher Hitchens, *The Trial of Henry Kissinger* (London: Verso, 2001), 55.

3. Hitchens, *The Trial of Henry Kissinger*, 56.

4. Noam Chomsky, *Language and Politics*, ed. C. P. Otero (New York: Black Rose Books, 1988), 681.

5. Jonathan Schell, "The Lexicographers," *The Nation*, July 12, 2004, 10.

6. Schell, "The Lexicographers," 10.

7. Chomsky, *Language and Politics*, 673.

8. Cited in Donaldo Macedo, *Literacies of Power: What Americans Are Not Allowed to Know* (Boulder, Colo.: Westview Press, 1994), 9.

9. Chomsky, *Language and Politics*, 671.

10. Joan Vennochi, *Boston Globe*, June 17, 2003, A17.

11. "Private Study Estimates Iraq War Dead at 13,000," AFP, Oct. 28, 2003, 1.

12. Cited in *In These Times*, Dec. 8, 2003, 6.

13. Arundhati Roy, "The New American Century," *The Nation*, Feb. 9, 2004, 12.

14. Kate Holton, "The Father of an American Civilian Beheaded in Iraq Accused President Bush and the U.S. Media Tuesday of Ignoring the 'Horrible Face of War.'" London (Reuters), May 3, 2004.

15. James Carrol, "Millennial War," *Boston Globe*, June 17, 2003, A17.

16. Quoted in Schell, "The Lexicographers," 10.

17. Quoted in Schell, "The Lexicographers," 10.

18. Cockburn, "Green Lights for Torture," 9.

19. David Barsamian, "The Progressive Interview," *The Progressive,* May 2004, 37.

20. Barsamian, "The Progressive Interview," 37.

21. "Pentagon: US Frigate Attacked by Iraq in Gulf Possible Error Cited," *Boston Globe,* May 18, 1987, 1.

22. "Pentagon: US Frigate Attacked."

23. "Pentagon: US Frigate Attacked."

24. Barsamian, "The Progressive Interview," 36.

25. Robert J. Fields, *The History of the United States,* vol. 2 (New Jersey: Ammanour Corp. Book-Lab, 1987), 135.

26. James W. Gibson, *The Perfect War* (New York: Vintage Books, 1988), 146.

27. Cockburn, "Green Lights for Torture," 9.

28. Gibson, *The Perfect War,* 158.

29. Paulo Freire, *The Politics of Education* (South Hadley, Mass.: Bergin & Garvey, 1985), 116.

30. Tom Paxton, "What Did You Learn in School Today?" Copyright 1962, Cherry Lane Music Publishing Company, Inc.

31. Barsamian, "The Progressive Interview," 39.

32. Baruch Kimmerling, "The ICJ Ruling and Israel's Fence," *Boston Globe,* July 10, 2004, A11.

33. Gibson, *The Perfect War,* 202–3.

34. Cockburn, "Green Lights for Torture," 9.

35. Cockburn, "Green Lights for Torture," 9.

36. As cited in "Quayle, in Boston, Tells of U.S. Relief Effort for Iraq Refugees," *Boston Globe,* Apr. 12, 1991, 15.

2
SCHOOLS AND THE MANUFACTURE
OF MASS DECEPTION: A DIALOGUE

᪣

MACEDO: In your 1967 book *Vietnam: The Logic of Withdrawal*, you called for an immediate withdrawal from Vietnam without any conditions. But of course that didn't happen, and we have learned that thousands and thousands of innocent victims, including women and children, could have been spared from the vicious violence unleashed by the U.S. military against the people of Vietnam that ranged from the wanton spraying of Agent Orange (a chemical warfare) to carpet bombing of civilians in densely populated areas, such as the bombing of Hanoi. Tragically, President Johnson did not adhere to your suggestions.

Now, here we are again, committing something that is fundamentally wrong in Iraq that revisionist historians will later whitewash as a mistake. In your recent piece published in *The Progressive*, you made a similar call for an immediate withdrawal from Iraq without any conditions, and you wrote a lovely and eloquent speech that could

---

This dialogue between Howard Zinn and Donaldo Macedo took place in January 2004 in Cambridge, Massachusetts.

have been given by any of the Democratic candidates for president—a speech based on the very democratic fabric upon which this nation was built, at least in theory. Most of the Democratic presidential candidates would not have the courage to develop a presidential campaign based on ideals of true democracy and social justice. But even if they did, their political handlers would summarily argue against adhering to the democratic propositions in your speech because, according to them, a progressive discourse that celebrates true democratic ideals such as equity, social and racial justice, and peace would constitute political suicide. In fact, this is precisely what happened to the candidacy of Howard Dean when the mass media strangled his presidential aspirations overnight because he raised too many impertinent questions concerning the illegal war in Iraq and talked about protecting the majority against the economic tyranny of the few. As you know, Howard Dean is hardly the ideal progressive candidate, and many of his proposals could be considered center right. Nevertheless, he was considered too radical for the establishment.

The paradox for me is why—in a society that embraces the myth of democracy to the point that the majority of Americans supported the illegal war against Iraq so we can undemocratically impose democracy—are politicians who truly want to create conditions for the actual practice of democracy along the lines proposed by the Declaration of Independence hardly taken seriously? In fact the political pundits would really argue against adhering to your position because they see your proposals for equity, democracy, and social justice as being either out of touch with reality or, worse, subversive socialist propaganda. It is to this huge contradiction that I want to turn our attention. Of course we have the propaganda state, the media, and so on working to "manufacture consent" and docility, but in our conversation today I would like to hear what you have to say regarding the role that schools play in creating this paradox and the mechanisms schools use to maintain it so as to reproduce dominant values that, ultimately, work counter to the very democratic ideals that schools seemingly promote. Do you see the contradiction?

ZINN: It's interesting. In a way the educational system, the schools, prepare young people to live with those contradictions and to accept them and to think they're OK. Because the schools give the people the ideals. The schools teach people about the Declaration of Independence, and they teach young people that we live in a democracy and that there is equality and justice for all. These are the ideals, you see. And then at the same time the schools do not give the young people, or even older people if they're in adult education programs, the information that shows how these ideals are being violated every day. So that, on the one hand, the schools give students the ideals, but, on the other hand, they don't give students the analytical tools so that they can look at society today and see what the discrepancy is between the ideals and the reality.

Or, to put it another way, the schools don't give students an accurate picture of reality. If they did, then the glaring difference between the ideals and the state of people in this society would be very apparent to students. For instance, schools do not give students a real picture of the class divisions in society. They don't give students a picture of how money dominates every aspect of society. Money obviously dominates the economic system, but it also dominates the political system, the culture, and even the educational system itself. Schools don't give students a look at how wealth and corporate power are dominant in this society, nor do they give their students a picture of how the other classes, the less-than-wealthy classes—that is, the

29

oppressed—live. Students do not get an accurate picture of homelessness, they don't get an accurate picture of how poor people live, they don't get an accurate picture of what it's like to be a tenant subject to the power of a landlord or what it's like to be an unemployed person looking for a job and being frustrated every day. They do not get a picture of what it is to be black, to be colored in this society—a real picture of what it's like—and that's why when students are given, for instance (this was my own experience), the *Autobiography of Malcolm X* to read, they are startled. Because it's such a vivid and compelling and personal story, they say, almost for the first time, "This is what it's like to be a black person in society." Before reading such a book, they have this idea, "Oh, yes, there's discrimination, segregation, and so on," but there are two ways of knowing something: you know something superficially or you know something that hits you in your gut. And it can hit you in your gut even if you are not a victim of it. If you yourself are a victim of it, you don't have to learn about it, you experience it. But if you are a white person living in society, it's possible for you to begin to feel what it's like to be a person of color. You don't know exactly what it's like, but you can at least begin to understand it. That's what literature does. People read Richard Wright's *Black Boy* or Ralph Ellison's *Invisible Man,* and it wakes them up to what it feels like to be black. So we have this enormous gap in our educational system, where young people learn about the ideals of liberty and democracy but they don't learn about the reality of a class society in which a very small number of wealthy people dominate the society and in which, at the other end of the spectrum, there are huge numbers of people who live on the edge of survival, who are really struggling to stay alive, to feed their kids, and to send their kids to school.

MACEDO: And the middle-class folks usually blame the loss of their jobs on immigrants, high taxes, and the welfare state, as they castigate the poor for the meager social assistance they might get from the government—the welfare queen syndrome catapulted to the national stage by former President Ronald Reagan. However, most of the same middle-class individuals who feel insecure economically are seldom able (or willing) to link their job losses to the corporate greed that makes them redundant through "outsourcing" (a euphemism for job liquidation) in order to generate greater and greater profits for corporations and their investors. Members of the middle class also fail to understand that our government has a hand in their misery because it promotes the exportation of jobs abroad by providing tax breaks and subsidies to corporations that do so.

It is for this reason that it becomes imperative for educators to help students shorten the gap between a superficial understanding of reality and the knowledge, as you put it, of "something that hits you in your gut." However, this is not an easy task, given the weight of dominant pedagogy designed primarily to domesticate and create obedient workers. For example, when I was teaching a course at the Harvard Graduate School of Education called "Anti-Racist Multicultural Education," a heated discussion ensued concerning the value of the METCO program—a program designed to bus a small number of inner-city students (primarily students of color) to suburban schools so they can have a better chance at a quality education. To provoke further analysis, I suggested to the class that we should also create a METCO program in reverse, where well-to-do white suburban students would be bused to inner-city schools so they can experience firsthand and understand the human misery and economic deprivation

31

of ghetto living. This class was made up of mostly well-intentioned, affluent, white women who had an interest in working in inner-city schools. However, with the exception of a small number of minority students, the majority of the students in the class saw no pedagogical value in my proposal. In fact, they perceived my proposal as contentious, provocative, and unworkable since most suburban parents would not allow their children to be bused into city schools. As one student noted, "that is why they fled to the suburbs in the first place." The reason that was given most often against busing rich, white students to inner-city schools was that these schools and the neighborhoods in which they are located are too dangerous. When I asked them whether these schools and neighborhoods are also dangerous for the poor and mostly nonwhite students trapped in them, they agreed but contended that my proposal would only inflame class warfare and controversy.

As you can see, it is OK, if not cool, to study poverty in elite and wealthy universities in order to later become managers of poverty, such as directors of Head Start programs and other social initiatives in the inner city, but it is altogether another matter to ask these same white, affluent students to allow themselves to be "hit in the gut" in order to truly learn what it means to experience deprivation, discrimination, and dehumanization. Many of the students in the class were part of the Risk and Prevention Program at Harvard, but they were unwilling to ask the simple question of who put these students at risk to begin with, nor were they interested in delving into the root cause of poverty and its social consequences.

ZINN: That is understandable if the class system in the United States is to remain invisible and the myth of a classless society intact. And your proposal to deconstruct the contradiction is even more threatening to what is called the middle class, since they also experience great alienation and insecurity. The middle class in this country is supposed to be the sign of America's prosperity; it is often pointed to as a sign of how successful capitalism is, because we have created a large middle class of people who have television sets, who have cars, who may even own their own homes, and so on. But what is not represented actively is the psychic insecurity of people in that class, because so long as there is a class society including both the very rich and the very poor, members of the middle class never know which way they are going. They never know whether their jobs will be there tomorrow because the middle class is not the ownership class. Even if they are professionals or run small businesses, members of the middle class live in a society where they are ruled by somebody more powerful than they are, and they can lose their livelihoods suddenly—we're seeing this now in the United States, where so many middle-class people are suddenly losing their jobs.

MACEDO: You are correct, and more and more this economic dislocation is breeding tremendous insecurity in a large number of middle-class people.

ZINN: For example, on my street there are three people who were earning very good salaries working in the computer industry, and suddenly all three of them are unemployed. And in the meantime they have contracted to build additions on their houses, they have bought more goods, and they have sent their kids to private schools. So suddenly the middle class is nervous and insecure in our class society. And there are ways, of course, of educating people about this. Some teachers do this; it can be done. But the educational system at large, in the main, does not educate students about the realities of living in a class society, and instead young people grow up thinking that this is a successful society and that the Horatio Alger myth still persists—that if you work hard and get educated, you will be prosperous and successful and, presumably, that then the ideal that you once learned about will have been obtained.

MACEDO: You made reference to class, which is one of the issues I was hoping that we could elaborate on in this dialogue. I am reminded of the conversation we had in the coffee shop in Harvard Square when your friend raised the issue of your role as a working-class intellectual. It amazes me that the vast majority of people in this society, including highly educated individuals, particularly in schools of education where teachers are prepared, continue to promote or to embrace the myth that we live in a classless society. When I read your piece *Being Left: Growing Up Class-Conscious* [chapter 7, this volume], I was incredibly touched and moved by your description of what it meant to grow up as a working-class kid, helping your dad, who was a waiter, during a New Year's Eve party. You helped him clear and clean the tables while the well-to-do enjoyed the celebration totally oblivious to what it meant for working-class folks to struggle because, by and large, the party-goers had never experienced working-class living conditions. Yet in most schools, even those teachers who grew up in the working class often find ways to block any substantive discussion concerning class analysis, and they often proceed to teach the myths of classlessness.

For instance, this myth of the classless society gets reproduced in the way we do research in education. The class variable is never really allowed because, according to pseudoscientist educators, it taints objectivity. Also, as you have mentioned earlier, we don't need to create an educational context where students begin to experience and explore what it means to be a part of the working class, what it means to be poor, and what it means to be homeless because the curriculum is about somebody else's reality; the educational objective in our schools is to assimilate everybody into a mythical middle-class ideal, even though most working-class students, particularly students of color, will never experience that promised middle-class reality. It's a form of colonialism in that the vast majority of working-class students are often betrayed by the promises of the school discourse. At most only a small percentage of students in each generation will truly enjoy the fruits of the ideal classless society promised by schools. The mechanisms used for the blind acceptance for class assimilation are not too dissimilar from the tools used by colonial powers to legitimize the disparity and the often inhumane conditions created by colonialism. In this respect, schools usually function to provide justification and legitimization of what would be otherwise considered inhumane, exploitative, and oppressive.

What do I want say about the role of education in the promotion of this myth of classlessness in the United States? Let me be specific. I came to the United States from Cape Verde, in West Africa, a colonial possession of Portugal marked by a cruel class division that bothered me from a very early age. When I immigrated with my family to the United States we took residence in Dorchester, Massachusetts, in 1966. I remember feeling a sense of relief, almost an acquired freedom, because around me, outside the racial factor that was generating elevated levels of tension in the neighborhood, everybody seemed to be in the same class. I really thought that yes, the myth is true, in the United States there is no class. But what I did not realize until I went to college is that growing up in Dorchester I did not have access to the middle- and upper-class reality. I didn't experience class distinctions in the United States until I went to college and some of my professors began to invite me over to their houses in Newton, Brookline, and Lexington, which are mostly white, middle- and upper-class echelons. Because I was locked into a working-class reality without realizing it, I had made the generalization that everybody is equal in terms of class, because I couldn't really conceive otherwise. Yes, there were rich people, but I believed that they didn't belong to a separate class, because we are all the same. After all, we all had televisions and cars, although ours was of an inferior model. And as I mentioned earlier, it took a graduate program to wake me up to the class reality in the United States. I find it fascinating that the system is able to engage us in the pedagogy of lies to the point that even educators, who should know better, continue to promote the false notion of a classless society even when the reproduction of this myth produces dire consequences for working-class students, such as providing them with a rationalization for their school failures through academically crafted deficit theories.

ZINN: It's interesting. When I think of my own education, there was nothing in it that talked about class differences, and of course all the symbols of early education are the kinds of symbols that dominate our culture: the flag, the Pledge of Allegiance, America, the words, the language. And it's always as if we all belong to one class. You're aware, even if you grow up in a working-class community, that somehow, somewhere in the distance—you see their pictures in the papers, or you see them on the screen, in the news—there's a rich class. But you actually don't think of, and nothing in your education prepares you for, the fact that there is some connection between their wealth and your poverty. You're never asked to question, never led to question how it is that some people are rich and others are poor. To put it another way, you're taught to accept what is there, you're not taught to challenge what is there, you're taught to believe that this is all natural. It is natural that you should live this way, it is natural that some should live that way, there's no criticism of that and nobody raises the question of how it has come to be this way or raises the question of whether it can be different. I never assumed growing up that it could be different. I wasn't even led to think about it.

MACEDO: And if you begin to feel victimized by this "natural" order supported by a commonsense folk theory, the message then is "it's your own fault . . . if you work hard enough, you will get the goodies like everyone else."

ZINN: It begins in the elementary schools. When I went on from elementary school to junior high school to high school—all of this was in the working-class milieu—the educational system taught about the Founding Fathers and the Constitution, and it taught us pride in the American Revolution and the Civil War, the great presidents and the great military leaders. There was nothing in my education that suggested that there was anything wrong with the existing arrangements. And what was missing from my education was this: any notion that in addition to great presidents and military heroes in our history there were also dissidents, people who rebelled. Of course I never learned that there were mutineers in George Washington's army in the Revolutionary War, or about the class nature of the draft riots during the Civil War. I certainly never learned—because it was always very simple, the Confederacy was bad, the North was good— that in the Confederacy there was class conflict, that poor people deserted from the Confederacy, that the wives of soldiers in the Confederacy rioted in Georgia against the plantation owners who were growing cotton instead of food because it was more profitable. There was no class consciousness in any of my education, and this continued right up into college and graduate school. There was no notion at all, you see, that it was possible to live in a different way. So all of my education was kind of Machiavellian, that is, the schools taught that this is the way things are and therefore you have to be pragmatic and realistic and just be part of this system the way it is. Because you don't learn about people who question the system, because you haven't been given a reason to question the system, because you haven't been asked what causes these class differences, and you haven't been given a larger picture of class segmentation in society, even if you know your own background and your background was poor. So that you live in some small part of the country and that is what you know, but you don't generalize from that and you don't see how this is a social phenomenon, a national phenomenon, so you don't think about this in larger terms.

I'm trying to think of whether anywhere in my education, right up until graduate school, I was given any notion of class conflict and class struggle in society. There were little hints of it. You'd be told about a particular labor struggle very superficially, such as the Pullman strike of 1894. You were only told about that, really, because Eugene Debs was involved in it and he was a presidential candidate. Anybody who was a presidential candidate was important because the one thing that you were socialized in was to believe in the importance of elections and to pour all of your civic energy into elections. So somebody who ran for president, OK, he was important so we give him a little attention. But the great labor struggles of the United States are glossed over or ignored completely. Actually, the United States has a history of some of the most dramatic labor struggles; it is one of the most amazing stories in Western history, but that history was absent from my education right up through graduate school. And so if I hadn't gone out and looked for it on my own and been led to it because of my own background, not just as a working-class person but specifically as a young, radical, working-class person (because that made a difference, you know) I never would have learned about those dramatic labor struggles. I could have been a working-class person and simply put that behind me, but as a young, working-class person who read Marx, Upton St. Clair, Jack London, Lincoln Stephens, and so on—as a young working-class person who read about other possibilities—I looked in my courses for class conflict and didn't find it. So I went out and looked for it myself. When I was an undergraduate at New York University, there was nothing in the history classes about the great labor struggles. I had to create an individual program for myself, and I found an advisor who would accept this, and then I could go ahead and read about the great strikes in American history. But I had to go out of my way to do this on my own because the educational system didn't give me any of that.

MACEDO: This control of the curriculum that leads to selective erasure of history continues today in the false promotion and reproduction of the myth that the United States is a classless society where everybody is the same. What I find paradoxical is the failure of the labor movement, particularly of the Left, to fill the gap, since the educational system is partly a function of a white, middleclass reality designed to reproduce values in the service of the dominant ideology. Why is it that the labor movement, or the Left for that matter, did not exercise a greater influence by teaching and creating conditions that would provide critical tools or avenues to find the information not available to students, particularly those students who yearn to think otherwise? We are then left to find out about these things when we have grown up. I read last night, for instance, what you wrote about the fact that you discovered the bad and criminal side of Columbus only after you finished your Ph.D.

ZINN: That's right.

MACEDO: It's amazing that you can earn a Ph.D. and do historical work while continuing to perpetuate the myth of Columbus as the good guy, the great hero, ignoring the atrocities, the massacres that he committed. Where do you see the disjunction happening in this great labor struggle and its inability to penetrate into schools to make them more democratic, more open, and more accessible? Do you see where I'm trying to go in terms of the failure of the labor movement to influence schools?

ZINN: I see where you go. It's a difficult question, because going back in history to the trade union movement, the American Federation of Labor, which was the most powerful labor union in the United States between the 1880s and the 1930s, was not interested particularly in this kind of class-oriented history. The American Federation of Labor consisted of skilled workers who had been successful in the system and who were taught to be very narrowly concerned with their own conditions and their own wages, not concerned with people outside their trades or crafts, not concerned with unskilled workers, immigrant workers, blacks, or women. And so the idea of a class-oriented education didn't mean anything to members of the American Federation of Labor, because in a sense they represented a certain class of privileged workers who did not have a larger view. Now there were trade unions in the history of the United States that did have a larger view—

the Industrial Workers of the World (IWW), for instance, but the IWW was never able to penetrate or have any connection with the U.S. educational system. Remember, until the end of World War II and until millions of working-class guys entered the educational system under the GI Bill, the educational system after elementary school was closed to most working-class people. After laws were passed to provide a high school education to everybody, you know what happened: working-class students usually got the worst possible schools.

MACEDO: Well, that's what happened to you—you benefited from GI Bill assistance to further your schooling. Was this also a form of affirmative action?

ZINN: Yeah, exactly. But the educational system was a very limited system, and the IWW had no connection with that world of education. The people who were in the IWW might have been educated themselves, self-educated, but that never penetrated into the formal educational system. When the Congress of Industrial Organizations (CIO) was formed in the 1930s, it began to organize unskilled workers, black workers, and women workers and to organize the mass industries of the 1930s, auto and rubber. At that point you had for the first time a connection between radicalism and the labor movement and the idea of education; that is, a number of the unions, particularly left-wing unions of the 1930s, set up educational programs. These unions had education directors, and the National Maritime Union had an educational program that was led by left-wing people, first the son of Daniel De Leon, who was an important socialist of the nineteenth century, and then Leo Huberman, who was a left-wing writer of history and economics, and they carried on educational programs for their members. There are still vestiges of that today; Local

1199 in New York still carries on educational and cultural programs. But that was always a separate educational system within the union, and it only involved a relatively small number of union members and never really penetrated the formal educational system.

Now why is this?

MACEDO: Yes, that's the question.

ZINN: Why is this? I've been dodging that question because I don't know the answer, except to say that the educational system was resistant to that kind of knowledge. I mean, how could the labor movement have an impact on schools? It could only happen if people in the educational system saw what was going on in the trade union movement, looked at these educational programs, and said, "oh, we need that as part of education." But no, the educational system has always been dominated by people who are not looking for change, who do not want to acknowledge the U.S. class system, who are looking for safety. Taking pointers from the labor movement would not have been a safe thing for schools to do. People in the educational system, like middle-class professionals anywhere, are very concerned about their security, their safety; they're subject to people above them. They're not of the upper rungs in the hierarchy of authority, so they worry about their standing and what can happened to them, and therefore they have admissions standards to the educational system. They don't want to rock the boat, they don't want to draw attention to themselves.

We're sitting here in the offices of the Trade Union Program of Harvard University. The Trade Union Program brings together union leaders from all over the country and even other parts of the world. They get together for eight-week periods, and they discuss all sorts of important things. It's an education, a real education here, for union people. They bring these trade union people here, and they bring Noam Chomsky, and they bring economists, and they bring even me in, and it's a concentrated educational thing for trade unionists. It's a totally separate thing from Harvard University. The students at Harvard University do not know of the existence of this program.

MACEDO: I never knew about the existence of this program until today. However, I am not a bit surprised that Harvard University would keep this program a secret and that most students don't know about its existence. On the other hand, this program functions also to promote the myth of academic freedom, openness, and rigorous inquiry espoused by Harvard in its promotional literature.

ZINN: Yeah, you were in the schools of education, and here we are, like we're in a prison cell and they won't allow visiting hours. And this is the way it's been. The world of education is its own world, it does not want outsiders, it has immigration restrictions. It doesn't want people who will trouble the system, who will get in the way of turning out people whose one aim is to become successful in America in some way. And if you rock the boat, if you introduce troubling questions about the system, they're not ready for this, they won't accept this.

MACEDO: Do you think that this form of educational domestication also could be part of the reason that led to my initial question to you—why was the labor movement not aggressive enough to infiltrate in order to help transform education? Could it be that the movement itself, perhaps, was not quite willing to challenge the basic principle of capitalism? In other words, the labor movement was unwilling to transform and envision a society beyond capitalism. Instead, the labor movement focused mostly and narrowly on the need to make the lot of workers better and to share minimally the profits generated through their labor. The movement never intended to raise questions concerning the control of means of production, to raise issues regarding ownership, or to promote racial, class, and gender equity. These challenges would have to be met squarely and promptly but, unfortunately, this did not occur. The underlying belief is that you don't really want to educate young radicals who would push the envelope of social justice and equity and go beyond the narrow proposals set forth, a priori, by a labor movement that had an aversion toward any socialist-sounding proposals to begin with. Could this be a partial explanation for the narrowness of the labor movement in the United States?

ZINN: No question. I was dealing with one half of it. That is, here are these two entities, here is the educational system and here is, you might say, a class-oriented view of the world, which you find in some parts of the labor movement, and the two don't come together. And I was just talking about how the educational establishment itself closes the door to that. But what you were just talking about is the other side of it, that is, that the labor movement itself has had such a narrow vision. . . .

MACEDO: That's my point. One could also add that, in certain moments, the labor movement had no vision at all outside the struggle for a modicum of reform to better the working conditions of workers (not all workers, especially not ethnic and racial workers) and to secure a modest share of the profit generated through their labor. The labor leadership never sought to exercise substantive control over the means of production and promote issues of social justice and social welfare for all workers regardless of race, ethnicity, gender, and creed.

ZINN: The labor movement in the United States has had such a narrow vision. You know, in Britain the Labour Party at least called itself a socialist party, it accepted the idea of socialism. In many countries in the world, trade union movements are radical in their orientation; socialist, anticapitalist, they have deep critiques. In the United States, you might say that the labor movement—except for that brief period of the IWW in the early twentieth century and except for a small number of the unions in the CIO, some of which were destroyed by the 1950s. During the cold war, with the emergence of the McCarthy period and the promulgation of the Taft-Hartley Act that enabled unions to purge communists and radicals, the trade union movement in the United States purged itself of left-leaning leaders in order to ingratiate itself with the establishment and to move closer to the seat of power. The trade union movement went along with purging those unions and those union leaders who had a larger vision, a class-conscious vision of society. So I mean the problems, yes, are not just the obstacles set up by the educational system but also the limitations of the trade union movement in the United States. Of course that raises a difficult question, which is why the trade union movement in the United States is so limited in its vision as compared to those of other countries. And one possible answer is that the United States, with all its wealth, has been able to, you might say, bribe a certain section of the working class, giving it just enough privilege, just enough benefits to make the trade union movement collaborators with the system and so the incentive for trade unions to present a broader vision has not been there because they felt that we can do all right within the system. And the answer was, yes, some of them could do all right within the system, a minority, but in addition, the trade union movement of the United States has always been a minority of the working class. There are other countries in which a much larger percentage of the working class belongs to trade unions. In France, 80 percent of the workers belong to some trade union. In the United States, it never exceeded 30 percent, and now it's down to 10 percent, 12 percent. So yes, in the United States, the trade union movement itself has had a very limited vision, and the most potentially radical workers, the most potentially radical and troublesome members of the working class, have generally been outside the trade union movement, and that's certainly true today.

MACEDO: The creation of this accommodated class of laborers, who were given certain privileges (one could argue bones to chew on) due to the immense resources and wealth of the United States, anesthetized the labor movement's ability to connect with, for instance, our foreign policy, which has always been designed to exploit workers from poor and underdeveloped countries, thus enabling U.S. society to maintain and enjoy a higher standard of living. The exploitation of both workers and natural resources in other countries provides the U.S. market with the means to provide its workers with some privileges, albeit limited ones, not enjoyed by workers from the countries that are being exploited. The ability to maintain a higher standard of living within the United States functions as a form of co-optation of U.S. workers, who then become complacent and indifferent to the imperialistic exploitation of third-world workers, including children. If, on the other hand, schools would provide students with the critical tools to make the necessary linkages in order to better comprehend a particular reality and its raison d'être, the level of complacency and indifference on the part of U.S. citizens toward the suffering of third-world people would, perhaps, drastically change.

Take, for example, high school teacher Bill Bigelow's use of a soccer ball in his global studies classroom, designed to encourage students to read multiple realities linked with the ball. Bigelow began the lesson with a beat-up soccer ball and asked students to write a description. As expected, he was greeted with "puzzlement and annoyance" because, according to one student, "it's just a soccer ball." The students' "accounts were straightforward and accurate if uninspired."[1] Although Bigelow's students provided an accurate description of the ball, their depictions remained purely physical, with little connection to a "deeper reality associated with this ball—a reality that advertising and consumption-oriented rhythms of U.S. daily life discouraged students from considering, 'Made in Pakistan.'"[2]

Bigelow then invited his students to inquire about the "human lives hidden in 'just a soccer ball'—a clue to the invisible Pakistanis whose hands crafted the ball."[3] Aware of the importance of making linkages, Bigelow used Bertolt Brecht's poem "A Worker Reads History" to engage his students in a deeper meaning contained in the hidden stories of the soccer ball:

> Each page a victory
> At whose expense, the victory ball?
> Every ten years a great man,
> Who paid the piper?

By using Brecht's poem, Bigelow eclipsed the criticism alleging that the development of political clarity politicizes education and invariably waters down the curriculum. Who would argue that reading Brecht waters down education? After reading the poem, Bigelow asked his students to "re-see" the soccer ball. Students raised questions: Who made this soccer ball? Where did the real people go after the ball was made? One student, Sarah, wrote: "I sew together these shapes of leather. I stab my finger with my needle. I feel a small pain, but my fingers are so callused. Everyday I sew these soccer balls together for 5 cents, but I've never once had a chance to play soccer with my friends. I sew and sew all day long to have these balls shipped to another place where they represent fun. Here, they represent the hard work of everyday life."[4]

When we compare the first description of the soccer ball that focused on accurately describing the physical properties of the ball with Sarah's in-depth reading of the world of exploitation and suffering contained within the soccer ball, we see how political clarity not only expands the range of possibilities for making meaning but also improves the quality of writing. Sarah's understanding that her privilege comes at the high cost of someone else's sweat and suffering enabled her to develop the necessary empathy that could easily lead to action against all forms of oppression and exploitation. What Bill Bigelow's lesson shows is that it is possible to imagine a better world and that new pedagogical structures can be created where students become critical agents rather than mere objects to be filled with official myths and ideas. Then it is not a coincidence, nor is it innocent, that both schools and trade unions in the United States neglect to make the necessary linkages that could unveil the inherent exploitative nature of capitalism. The development of critical tools to make linkages to better comprehend the world would necessarily unveil U.S. imperialism, even though after the invasion of Iraq imperialism is now presented in the mass media as a national goal while the majority of the citizenry remains indifferent to its ramifications and consequences.

ZINN: But of course that failure to make connections to other countries is true in the trade union movement, and it's even more true in the educational system. Though I must say in the trade union movement we are beginning to see a small breakthrough with the globalization issue— we're beginning to see that because, for the first time, workers are looking at what's happening to them domestically, and they're having to confront our connections with foreign workers and to see, for instance in Mexico, that the free trade agreement has been hurtful both to Mexican workers and to American workers, and so they're the seeds of solidarity. And we now see that there is a global movement; along with the globalization of the great economic powers, there's a globalization of resistance, and we now see international gatherings, the World Social Forum, which met in Porto Alegre, Brazil, as well as Seattle, Washington. The people participating in this globalization of resistance are still the minority, of course, still a small minority, but it's the beginning of consciousness about the connection between class exploitation here and class exploitation in other countries. But in the educational system it hasn't even gone that far. Probably the most egregious, the most flagrant failure in the American educational system, even beyond what I spoke about before, the failure to talk about class in the United States, has been the failure to understand the relations between the United States and other countries in the world, that is, American foreign policy. And the thing you pointed to, about the connections between the goodies that Americans can get, even the small goodies that Americans can get at the expense of workers in other countries, and W. E. B. Du Bois. . . .

MACEDO: He's one of the first American intellectuals to have raised this issue and it cost him dearly, forcing him to seek exile in Africa. The doctrinal reward system makes sure that dissent and a language of critique are not tolerated, and the cost of dissent, particularly a critique of capitalism, is usually very high, including one's life, as was the case with Martin Luther King Jr. The effectiveness of the doctrinal reward system to muffle dissent was painfully displayed after the 9/11 attacks, when all pretense of political opposition and critique in the United States just collapsed. Criticizing Bush administration policies for the war against Iraq was viewed as un-American. Members of Congress, including the Democratic opposition, understood that criticizing the president would have raised exponentially the possibility of their losing the next election. Thus, Congress became a rubber stamp to ratify all the policies on the conservative agenda, including tax cuts that benefited mostly the rich, while the distinction between the Republicans and Democrats simply disappeared.

ZINN: Yeah, that's right. W. E. B. Du Bois raised that issue and unfortunately we don't have a Du Bois in Congress now. And it's sort of natural that a black intellectual would raise that issue; after all, the relations between whites and blacks in the United States was a microcosm of the relations between Americans and people in other parts of the world because you might say that some white workers were benefiting from exploitation of black people in this country and Du Bois could see that connection. But the educational system teaches nothing about American foreign policy, teaches nothing that would suggest a critical look at American foreign policy. I mean, the general effect of the teaching of foreign policy, and this goes right up through graduate school, is to say that the United States has been a force for good in the world, basically that's the idea. There may have been a few aberrations, a few things. . . .

MACEDO: These aberrations are later whitewashed as mistakes, as McNamara described the Vietnam War. McNamara and other policy hawks would never admit that what they call "mistakes" constitute a wrong—a violation of international law and, in some cases, outright crimes against humanity, as was the case in Vietnam with the My Lai Massacre, even though the perpetrators of these crimes are seldom punished for their crimes. These same war hawks and policy makers would have no difficulty identifying these crimes against humanity and violations of international law if a country that they considered to be a "rogue nation" committed them. They would also have no qualms calling for the fullest application of the law. In fact, they might even recommend that the United States invade these "rogue nations" to indict these criminals, as was the case with Noriega when the United States invaded Panama. Never mind that Noriega was a thug and drug dealer created by the United States and protected and paid for years by the CIA.

ZINN: Exactly. That's right. In fact I was listening to, maybe you heard it too, an interview of the guy who made the film about McNamara, and the interviewer asked the film-maker, "Well, did you ask McNamara about the Vietnam War?" And the filmmaker said, "Well, McNamara admits there were some mistakes." It's all mistakes, you see, and not something that's inherent in the system and persistent throughout our policy. But this critical examination of American foreign policy is absent. You can see this most flagrantly in the lack of education about Latin America. I mean, I didn't even think about this until I got out of graduate school, it didn't occur to me that I'd learned nothing about Latin America. There was a required one-year course for history majors on the history of England, but nothing in the curriculum, required or not required, on our relations with Latin America. I mean, you would think, here are black students, well, what about Haiti, the first black republic? No, you could graduate after four years at a black college, and you'd never know that Haiti existed.

MACEDO: But we should not be at all surprised. After all, these countries are banana republics that we invade from time to time in order to whip them into shape to fend off altruistic and dangerous aspirations of sovereignty, social justice, and democratic ideals.

Linked to the absence of Latin America in the curriculum of U.S. schools is the total omission of analysis of the School of the Americas, and if one were to use President Bush's criteria in determining what constitutes a terrorist organization, one would have to classify this school as a terrorist training ground not too dissimilar to Osama bin Laden's, where Latin America's worst thugs and criminals were trained to commit the most horrendous crimes against their own populations (mostly civilians), such as the case with the slaughter of the Jesuit priests in El Salvador. But since these thugs were our thugs (these characterizations are never used by the administration, or the media, for that matter, to refer to these criminals; in fact, former President Reagan used to call them freedom fighters), not only are they never punished for their crimes and atrocities but also they are often rewarded. For example, Roberto D'Aubuisson, who as a major architect and sponsor of death squads in El Salvador was responsible for the assassination of Archbishop Oscar Romero and was also implicated in the slaughter of the Jesuit priests, was given red-carpet treatment in Congress by former Senator Jesse Helms of North Carolina. Can you imagine American reaction if Cuba, or any other country for that matter, hosted a high official from al Qaeda? It was no secret that both the Reagan and Bush administrations were heavily involved in the civil war in El Salvador by supporting the ultra-right political faction and its death squads, which were responsible for all kinds of barbarous atrocities committed mostly against civilians. The civil war casualty count in El Salvador is approximately thirty thousand dead. For these victims and their relatives, our support of this unjust and cruel war is no less terrorism than the vicious tragedy in New York on 9/11.

ZINN: Yeah, but you knew nothing about that. Americans could not, after graduating from college, tell you where Ecuador was or whether Guatemala was in the Western Hemisphere or in Africa. They couldn't tell you that. So the educational system brings up whole generations of American who do not understand what we have done to other countries. I must say that—and I haven't talked about this at all, because I have only said negative things about our educational system, and I'll continue, of course—since the 1960s we have begun to have a sort of smattering of people coming into the educational system with a broader social view, and people are teaching about Latin America—you know, somebody teaching at a privileged college like Wellesley who has been in Central America and has a progressive point of view about it—and African studies programs are just beginning. So we have now a small minority of teachers in the educational world, on the college level at least, I'm not even sure it's gotten into the high schools, who are beginning to teach something critical about American foreign policy. But in the main? No, Americans do not learn about this, and of course what this does is it leads Americans to accept uncritically what their government tells them about current foreign policy.

MACEDO: But they do this even when the evidence points to the contrary, which is really amazing. The last time we met, we talked about the fact that some 60–odd percent of college students continued to believe that Iraq had something to do with 9/11, even when President Bush himself has denied publicly such links and intelligence agencies all over the world have also come to the same conclusion. This shows you the power of the propaganda state, on the one hand, and, on the other, the total lack of critical thinking found in schools to counterbalance the propaganda apparatus. And this is very dangerous; it does not really bode well for the democratic ideals to which we claim to aspire. It also shows a high level of domestication that turns students into obedient automatons who eagerly move according to the marching orders given by the doctrinal system.

ZINN: I'm not surprised that 60 percent of college students would think something like the linkage between al Qaeda and Iraq is absolutely true, because they didn't get anything in their education that would prepare them to look critically at what the government says, so they listen to the government say again and again and again that something is true or hint and suggest and make connections, and then when the president denies it in one statement, it's not enough to penetrate what has already become a mountain of lies. I suppose it's encouraging—but then again, I'm easily encouraged, one might say desperate for encouragement—that *only* 60 percent of college-educated people believe that, since from what they get from the educational system, it should be 95 percent. So it means that there is, despite the educational system and despite the propaganda system, a countervailing network of underground information in this country that somehow seeps through to a fairly large number of Americans. And that is some cause for hope, because it shows that it may be possible to break through this control. In fact that possibility was realized during the Vietnam War, because during the Vietnam War, certainly, the educational system gave students no information, no background, on Vietnam. You could graduate from college and have no idea where Vietnam was. . . .

MACEDO: Neither did they have any idea about the cruel and violent U.S. policy toward Vietnam.

ZINN: And certainly nothing about our policy toward Vietnam. And what happened is that at the beginning of the Vietnam War, two-thirds of Americans supported the Vietnam War, and a few years later two-thirds of Americans opposed the war. What happened in between to make that change? Not the government, not the press. What happened in between was the effects of what I call the underground network, the counterculture, the underground newspapers, the community radio stations, the teach-ins, the rallies, the work of small radical groups (even though they did not have the major means of communication at hand)—the power of the truth was so strong that it overcame the government and media propaganda machines and reached a large number of Americans. So I'm suggesting that it wasn't the educational system itself that did it. The fact that we had to have teach-ins is a sign of that. What did the 1960s produce? Not only teach-ins but also alternative little schools within a school; we even had programs—voluntary programs, extracurricular programs—that were set up by the students themselves to teach about what was going on in the world because they couldn't get that information in their regular classes.

MACEDO: You mentioned this counterculture, and, of course, it gets manifested at least at the university level as ethnic studies, women's studies, African American studies, and so on, and these developments are great—no question in my mind—for a more pluralistic, multicultural society. And because these university developments often question the doctrinal systems, such as the interrogation of patriarchy by feminists, they are often under attack. In fact, the backlash is real. For instance, at the University of Massachusetts, where I teach, the College of Public and Community Services (CPCS), which is a community-oriented, highly progressive college, is currently under assault by the present university administration, which always points to the low enrollments as justification to withdraw resources from the college. Because CPCS now lacks adequate resources for recruitment, you end up with a vicious cycle that will progressively strangle it. One senior administrator at the university who shows a total distaste for CPCS and the democratic values it espouses, which are rooted in the ideals of the 1960s, remarked, "The problem with CPCS is that it is stuck in the Sixties vision of social justice and students are mostly interested in jobs"—which means that social justice in our society, which was founded on democratic ideals of social justice, is now considered something outdated and passé. So if CPCS wants to really get on with the program, it has to abandon its social justice orientation, which includes community programs that study issues of homelessness, housing for the poor, and other social issues that are very much pertinent for the underclass residents of Roxbury, Dorchester, and other economically depressed areas near Boston. It amazes me that an educator or an administrator in an urban and public educational system that was created with the primary goal of working toward social justice for the oppressed citizens of Boston and the surrounding areas would think that social justice is passé. It is scary, but that is a fact. So, although I am hopeful on the one hand, on the other hand there are tremendous obstacles that present real and difficult challenges for those of us who yearn to imagine a world that is less discriminatory and more just.

ZINN: Although the challenges, as you said, are difficult, it is important to think that change is possible, and we should remain always hopeful.

MACEDO: I wanted to ask you a question that I had also asked Paulo Freire many years ago in New York, which points to another paradox. The United States is one of the wealthiest countries in the world; it has the largest resources for education, both private and public, it has the highest level of teacher training compared to any other country in terms of the amount of money and number of courses and degrees that we give in education, and yet it produces staggering failures like in New York. As I had asked Paulo, how does one reconcile the fact that all this wealth, all these material and technological advancements in education, and all of this training end up producing huge educational failures, particularly among minority students that sometimes reach unacceptable dropout rates? Freire sort of smiled at me and said, "Donaldo, don't be naive. What you are calling failure is the ultimate victory of the system, because the system was never designed to educate those who are failing to begin with." And then he asked me, "Who are those who are failing? They are your blacks, your working-class whites, your ethnic folks, your immigrants." I had never really thought of it in this light. What we call the failure question should basically really be inverted—we are talking about the victory of the system, and I've been thinking a lot about it lately. Let's take New York, for example, which spends billions of dollars to maintain a system that generates largely failure. We tolerate this blatant failure in education, but let's say we had the same rate of failure in health care. The society would not tolerate that. For instance, if the *Boston Globe* revealed on its front page that 57 percent of the patients admitted to Massachusetts General Hospital died, immediately administrators, politicians, and the society in general would be calling for blue ribbon commissions to study the problem. In fact Massachusetts General Hospital would be closed, because no one would go there. Yet, we are willing to spend billions of dollars to support an educational system that generates failure, and nobody really cares. Again, we shouldn't be surprised since most of the white, middle- and upper-class students in Boston don't go to the Boston public schools anyhow. Do you see my point?

ZINN: Yeah. Of course the only reason the people on top would care in your example about the health care system is because people in the larger society would be rebellious against such extreme health care failure. And the question is, why aren't people in the larger society rebellious against what is happening in the educational system?

MACEDO: Because those who are victims of the educational system are considered to be disposable bodies who were never supposed to be educated in the first place. The ruling class would never tolerate dysfunctional educational programs for their children. That is why they pay large sums of money to send their children to private schools while they remain content that inner-city schools become containment centers for the underclass students who are, by and large, nonwhite. While the dominant class finds it unacceptable to, as they say, "throw more money" at educating poor, inner-city students (the Boston public school system spends approximately $8,000 per student per year), it has no difficulty bankrolling approximately $30,000 per person per year to contain a large percentage of the underclass "school dropouts" in jails. Perhaps they rationalize that $30,000 for each prisoner is a good investment in that it keeps a potentially large number of black and minority voters from exercising their right to vote, as was the case during the 2000 presidential election in Florida where thousands upon thousands of black voters were unfairly and illegally disqualified from voting. Jail will do the trick more easily, although it is more costly.

ZINN: Exactly. And it's a vicious cycle, because the people who are the victims of the system don't have the resources or the wherewithal to rebel against the system. Or their rebellion comes in another form: they go out into the streets, and they become dysfunctional people in society, and they're the ones who become the two million people in prison, or they're the ones who become the homeless. And they don't become an organized force. And the people who have the resources to resist and complain are the people whose children are the successful ones in the system. So it's representative of the larger problem in the society, which is true not only of education but also of the economy, and that is that the people who are the greatest victims of the economy—that is, the forty million people without health care, and the people who are unemployed, and the people who are living in the ghettos of the country—are the people who have the least resources to rebel. And every once in a while, of course, there is an upsurge, such as the riots of blacks in the 1960s; every once in a while there's something like that. The system puts them away, it puts them out of sight. And so the question is, at what point can there be a breakthrough in this? Will it require that the people who are successful in the system realize that they are not really successful, that they also will suffer from this, that the fact that there's an underclass undercuts the security of the people in the middle class? How and when this breakthrough will take place is very hard to say, because it's a kind of self-perpetuating system, and it will take something critical, troublesome, danger-ous—some crisis—to make people who think they are suc-ceeding in the system realize that they're not, that they are

succeeding in a system that ultimately makes them insecure. And I don't know the answer to breaking through
that kind of self-perpetuating cycle.

MACEDO: Which I think largely education promotes, sustains, and maintains in some direct way. This goes back to
the question that your friend raised during our conversation in the coffee shop in Harvard Square. Growing up
working class and being face-to-face with all kinds of dep-
rivations, humiliation, and alienation, as you discussed in
your essay that I read the other day, can you remain working class in the academy? I know that lots of working-class
folks who have "made it" then behave as if the system
functions justly and normally without much problem. My
friend Henry Giroux, who is also a friend of yours, once
told me very clearly when we were both teaching at Boston University that there's no such thing as a working-
class intellectual in the academy. According to him, if you
remain true to your working-class values, even in the way
you behave and the way you are in the world and with the
world, the academy will weed you out. And that's what
happened to him. In your case, you already had tenure so
John Silber couldn't get rid of you. But your presence,
and Henry's presence, along with the presence of others,
particularly those who are radicals and activists and whose
goal is to change the system, are not welcome in the academy; the academy imposes a level of censorship even while
claiming to espouse a free and open education.

And I wanted to ask you, in particular, about your relationship with John Silber, the former president of Boston
University, where you taught for many years. In my view,
John Silber behaved always like the ultimate fascist and
was, at the same time, always rewarded by the dominant
system with accolades from the *New York Times,* the *Boston
Globe,* and other media outlets that portrayed him as a

great educator, even though he's never written a book on education, and as a Kantian scholar, even though he wrote and published just two articles on Kant taken largely from his doctoral dissertation. The doctrinal system created a myth around him, elevating him to stardom, making him into someone who can go on television and dismiss scholars like you and Noam Chomsky—all the while providing no proof for his tirades and getting away with it. In fact, Silber was often rewarded for his falsehoods. Given this level of censorship of progressive thinkers in the academy, I am trying to grapple with how this works and how institutions of higher learning can promote people like John Silber, who bragged about having kept the Frankfurt School of thought out of Boston University, eliminated studies dealing with sexual orientation, and attempted to weed out all progressive thinkers (labeled leftists) from the faculty while spouting platitudes about scientific rigor in the pursuit of truth. Of course, it is his own version of the pursuit of scientific knowledge and democratic ideals. Can you talk about a society that enables people like John Silber to be who they are and rewards them and promotes them to the highest levels?

ZINN: After all, who has the controlling voice in universities? It's not the faculty, it's not the students, it's certainly not the janitors, the cleaning people, the secretaries; it's the trustees of the universities, or the boards of regents. And who are these people? In the case of boards of trustees, they're businesspeople, in the case of boards of regents, they're still businesspeople, they're people in the upper reaches, very often they're not people who have much to do with education. They're people who have political connections, people who have business connections, and they are the people who make the important decisions in the university. They decide who will be the president of the university. Ultimately they can decide which professors get tenure and which do not.

We go into the university naïvely, thinking it is a different place than the rest of society, an oasis; even if we have a critical view of society, the university is an oasis within this society. And I've known even radical people in the university who saw the university that way. Therefore in the 1960s, when people rebelled against the university they said, "You're destroying *our* university." I remember specifically a professor at Boston University who considered himself a Marxist saying, "Remember, it's our university." But it was never our university. So there's this naïveté about the university. But the university has always really been a part of the capitalist world in microcosm, controlled by business, controlled by people who have power and wealth and who make the ultimate decisions. And so it's possible for radical professors to occasionally make their way into the system and stay there and get tenure, but there are two things to note about them: one, there are not that many of them, and two, they can be used as examples of the tolerance of the system, of how democratic the system is. If Chomsky says the educational system is an undemocratic system, you can say, well, *you're* there, you have a position at MIT. Well, it's perfectly attuned to the American system of control, a very sophisticated system of control that allows just enough dissidence so that those in power can point to the fact that the university is democratic but not enough dissidence to create a real danger to the system. And so it operates like the world outside, with the same hierarchy of power, with the same bare margin of toleration for some people. And, at the same time, while some people, some radicals who become embedded in the system, you might say, retain their radicalism and teach in a different way and become active in outside political activities, there are many people who start out as radicals, enter the system, and while holding on to their reputations as radicals remain radicals only on a very abstract intellectual level. They might even teach a course in Marxism, but they are not dissidents—they are not dissidents in the society outside, and they are not dissidents in the university because they consider themselves part of the university and they hold to the idea, and therefore perpetuate the idea, that the university is basically a decent institution.

MACEDO: These are the intellectuals that Chomsky often refers to as "commissars," because ultimately their major function is to legitimize and reproduce those very values that, as intellectuals, they should work against. This leads to my last question. What do you see as the role of intellectuals not only in universities but also in K–12 education, since, in the view of many progressive thinkers, teachers are, or should be, first and foremost intellectuals who must also always be vigilant and willing to critique any form of social injustice? Teachers must also courageously work toward conditions that promote a society that is less dehumanizing and more humane. How can we accept the label *intellectual,* when in fact one is unable to ethically intervene to ameliorate a wrong? With rare exceptions of courageous and coherent intellectuals like you, Noam Chomsky, bell hooks, and Henry Giroux, among others, the vast majority of professors seem to cling to the naïve notion, as you put it, that "it's our system," "it's our school," "it's our university," even though these institutions do not belong to us. Intellectuals should always aim for a world that rejects all forms of dehumanization while celebrating the liberation of all people, regardless of race, religion, ethnicity, and gender. What can you say about the role of intellectuals in the United States and their obvious complicity with the power structure as they, through their work, end up legitimizing values that are unjust, exploitative, undemocratic, and, in final analysis, unethical?

ZINN: Well, the chief problem is that if intellectuals who do have a radical vision of this society, and who even present that vision in the education system in their teaching through the books they assign or what they say in their lectures, are not at the same time involved in the world outside, in the real social struggles that go on—if the classroom remains a sealed, intellectual entity—then they are teaching their students that this classroom radicalism is sufficient. They're teaching their students to be content with being intellectually dissident and then, maybe, to become teachers who will perpetuate the role of the intellectual dissident but without venturing into the world outside. . . .

MACEDO: Which is also a form of dilettantism.

ZINN: Yes, yes, certainly, a form of dilettantism. And in a way it's a marvelous way for the system to perpetuate itself, to contain dissent by giving people the illusion of being critics of the system without acting out that criticism in the society at large. And so for every radical social critic in the academy who is also out in the world acting out, exemplifying his or her ideas, there are many, many, many more radicals in the system who confine their radical critiques to the intellectual level and thereby teach passivity to their students. They teach contentment with the role they play, feeling that they are doing something important when actually they are perpetuating the barrier between the radical intellectual inside the university and the world outside. I know that every year there's a meeting in New York of socialist scholars. Several thousand people come, and I wonder how many of those several thousand people are actively involved outside of the academy, how many of them are just scholars, you see, and how many of them go outside. . . .

MACEDO: Well, the very label is telling—they're socialist scholars, and scholarship is not about engagement in action. So what you're saying, and I agree with you, is that reflection alone is not enough, and awareness alone is also not enough in that awareness must always be coupled with action, and action forces you outside the ivory tower. But this is also very much a class issue that informs and ultimately shapes the behaviors of many liberal professors. Many of these professors that you just described could even have a turbulent relationship with an activist like you because, at some level, they will feel threatened to the degree that your praxis becomes a mirror that shows their own complicity with the dominant system. That is, your praxis may make them realize that what they're doing is not sufficient and that their work is not part of a political project that collectively points to mechanisms to transform an unjust reality. In fact, their work would, invariably, reproduce the very dominant values they claim through their liberal discourse to interrogate. Unfortunately, it often ends up being a form interrogation without action. Furthermore, because they adopt a liberal discourse that accommodates rather than liberates, even when they teach, let's say, a course on Marxism, this fact is, in turn, used by the dominant institutions to say: "See, we are open and democratic, and we tolerate dissent."

NOTES

1. Bill Bigelow, "The Human Lives behind the Labels: The Global Sweatshop, Nike, and the Race to the Bottom," *Rethinking Schools* (1997): 1.

2. Bigelow, "The Human Lives behind the Labels," 1.
3. Bigelow, "The Human Lives behind the Labels," 1.
4. Bigelow, "The Human Lives behind the Labels," 12.

3
A PEOPLE'S HISTORY OF THE UNITED STATES

⊕

I'm going to talk about history. It's not hard to be a historian, really, you just study things that other people don't know, and then you tell them, and then you try to steer the conversation away from things they know. And you're a historian—it's simple.

I got into history for, I suppose, a very modest reason: I wanted to change the world. I didn't get into history— I mean I didn't really study history, go to college, do all of that—until I was about twenty-seven. By then I had worked at a shipyard for three years, I'd been in the Air Force, I'd knocked around at a number of different jobs—am I building up your sympathy? So by the time I came to study and teach history, I already had very strong views about the world, and I knew that history was important, and I guess that's the way I feel today. Not important in the way that very often you hear talked about, when politicians and sometimes educators talk about how young people don't

---

An earlier form of this essay was delivered as a lecture at Harvard University on February 17, 1999, as part of an Askwith Education Forum.

know history and then talk about the tests they gave young people and how they failed the tests. And these tests are devised, of course, by the people who called them ignorant.

I'm thinking of an incident a few years ago, when the *New York Times* tested a group of high school students as they do every few years to prove the ignorance of the high school students and the wisdom of people who give the tests. And then here's the *New York Times*, right? The summit, of . . . what? I guess the summit, it thinks, of American intellectual journalism. The kinds of questions posed about history to these students by the *New York Times* are questions like: Who was the president during the War of 1812? Who was the president during the Mexican War? What came first, the Homestead Act or the Civil Service Act? You recognize those questions, right? They're the kinds of idiotic questions that you get on the multiple-choice tests that determine whether you'll advance in your career. But are they important questions? The *Times* could have asked really important questions about the Mexican War instead of asking who was the president during the Mexican War.

In the United States we grow up in a quiz culture, where we're rated on the basis of how many of these kinds of questions we can answer. OK, Polk was president during the Mexican War, but it really doesn't matter who was president. There are more important things to know about the Mexican War, such as how did it start? Looking at that question would be really educational. Because then you would find that it started the way a lot of wars start, with a provocation and lies; in this case, the United States provoked the Mexicans by moving into disputed territory, an area between the Nueces River and the Rio Grande River, which both the Mexicans and the Americans claimed. The

American troops moved into this area, shots were fired back and forth, people were killed, and then President Polk announced to the country, "American blood has been shed on American soil." But of course he had planned a war with Mexico for some time; he had confided this to his diary. Of course, they didn't have tape recordings in those days, but we have ways of finding out these things. And so we went to war with Mexico and ended up with half of Mexico.

If you don't know important things about history, then it's as if you were born yesterday. And if you were born yesterday, then you will believe anything that is told to you by somebody in authority and you have no way of checking up on it. If you were born yesterday, then you will listen to the president get up before the microphones and the television cameras and say, "We must bomb Iraq." And if you knew some history, you might say, "Wait a while. Let me think about this." There have been other presidents who've said let's bomb here, let's bomb there, let's go there, let's invade here. And it very often turned out that behind those exhortations was a whole pack of lies. So while history might not tell you definitively what's the truth in this particular case, it at least teaches you to be cautious and skeptical. Or you might, I suppose, hear somebody say, "You know, affirmative action is wrong because it discriminates." Obviously, you're discriminating on behalf of black people, on behalf of women. And if you had no history—if you didn't know the history of affirmative action, if you didn't know the history of slavery, if you didn't know the history of discrimination, if you didn't know how many instances of affirmative action there have been in history, not for black people but, let's say, for rich people—you might look at it flatly in this one dimension and say yeah, affirmative action really is discrimination. I went to college under the GI Bill of Rights. I was a beneficiary of affirmative action. I was given special benefits to go to school, a special opportunity to go to school because I was a veteran. So there is a whole history of affirmative action in the United States, but now, finally, comes affirmative action for blacks and women, and many see this as new and bad.

If you were born yesterday, you'd be shocked by the knowledge that a president has lied. You would—it's astonishing! A president has lied! Now, if you knew some history . . . you wouldn't have to inspect very far. The lies told by presidents throughout history have been uncountable, you see. And if you go back just to World War II, go back just fifty years, you see Truman lying to the nation about the bombing of Hiroshima, saying we had bombed a military target. Or go back to Eisenhower. There are all sorts of lies, you know—concealment, deception, they're both degrees of lies. Sometimes liars take refuge behind one or another of those definitions. Like Eskimos have many different words for *snow,* politicians have many different words for *lies,* you see. But Eisenhower deceived a nation about what the United States was doing, secretly overthrowing the government of Iran in 1953 and overthrowing a democratically elected government in Guatemala in 1954. And he lied to the nation about the U-2 flights over the Soviet Union. What, us? We wouldn't do a thing like that. And the lying goes on and on. Kennedy and Johnson lied about the war in Vietnam. Kennedy lied about the Bay of Pigs. His lies, in fact, were prepared for him by a historian at Harvard University. Did you know that? Arthur Schlesinger briefed President Kennedy on how to respond to the press at the time of the Bay of Pigs, how to deceive them about the fact that the United States was involved in the invasion. In his memo to Kennedy,

Schlesinger wrote, "If lies must be told, it's better that they be told by subordinates." If you go back to Machiavelli's *The Prince*, you'll see that kind of advice given. We've had a lot of Machiavellis as advisors to presidents over the years. The lies come all the way down, of course, to Clinton. I don't mean lies about sex, I mean lies about important things. We bombed the Sudan because they're producing agents of chemical warfare and so on, but it turns out that there's no evidence for this, no evidence at all. Turns out that we bombed a medicine factory that produced half the medicines used by the people of the Sudan. These are important lies, these are matters of life and death.

So, yes, history can be trivial and history can be really important, depending on what you do with it and depending on what you learn. When I began to get involved in studying history, I knew immediately that I was not going to be what is called an "objective historian." I didn't believe in it; it became clear to me that there was no such thing as objectivity, that there's an enormous amount of hypocrisy in the history profession and elsewhere about objectivity. I saw that the very people who called for just telling the story as it is, telling the facts as they are and reproducing the past as it was, did history from their point of view. It seemed very clear to me; it didn't take much thought to realize that as soon as you do history you are confronted with the fact that you are selecting out of an infinite amount of data a certain amount of data, certain pieces of data, to include. And you make that selection according to your point of view, so that every historian and every work of history has a point of view. There's no such thing as a simple "fact." But in the past we've wanted our kids to know facts.

Do you remember Bob Dole? During the 1996 presidential campaign, Dole spoke to the American Legion.

While speaking about history—because Dole Knows History—Dole said our kids should learn facts, just facts, that they're getting too many interpretations, too many analyses. If you have read Dickens's novel *Hard Times,* you might remember a character named Gradgrind. He's a teacher—he's a caricature of a teacher, or at least I hope he's a caricature of a teacher. Gradgrind tells a younger teacher whom he's preparing, "Give your students just facts. Just facts." But Gradgrind is challenged by his own daughter, whom he's pushing into a marriage that she doesn't want. She says to him, "You know, Father, life is short." And he says, "I'm going to give you some facts. According to the Actuarial Tables, people in England live to a certain age. No, life is not short." And she says, "Father, I'm talking about my life." There's also the daughter of a circus performer who is in Gradgrind's class. Gradgrind is giving the class facts, facts, facts about how wealthy England is. And she speaks up and says, yes, but how much of this wealth is mine? That question is very pertinent to all of us living in the very wealthy United States. Because when somebody says, "We are doing well; the economy is great; the country is prosperous," the most important question for anyone to ask is, "How much of this wealth is mine? How much of this wealth belongs to these people? How much of this wealth goes here, and how much of this wealth goes there?"

So, I decided very early that everybody who does history does it from a point of view and selects the facts from a point of view, that you can't talk about something being a pure fact, because as soon as a fact is presented it is no longer purely a fact. As soon as a fact is presented, it represents a judgment. And the judgment that has been made is that this fact is important to present and other facts are not important to present. That's a very, very important judgment. And that's what the whole realm of historiography is about—deciding which facts are important and which facts are not important.

I was asked not long ago to participate in a symposium at Faneuil Hall on the Boston Massacre. I hesitated, and then I agreed to participate in the symposium so long as I didn't have to talk about the Boston Massacre. And they agreed. They figured, oh, we can have one odd person . . . let him do what he wants. It seemed very queer to me that the Boston Massacre was being presented as the most important massacre to have a symposium on, probably the only massacre to have a symposium on, right? Well as you know, Boston has this fixation on the American Revolution and everything connected with it. You know, half of the discussion about the Boston Massacre was about Paul Revere's engraving about the Boston Massacre. And to me it was a perfect example of how, out of a huge mass of really fascinating facts about American history, facts about massacres that have taken place in American history, this group focused on a massacre that barely fits the term, one of the least in terms of the number of people killed. You might say that this massacre got in just under the wire— if one person had stayed home in 1770, there would have been no symposium in the present day. Then I thought about other massacres in U.S. history. Has there ever been a symposium in Boston on the massacre of the Pequot Indians in New England in the 1630s, the burning to death of hundreds of people and the exaltation of the Puritan Fathers in that burning? Maybe there has been a symposium on it, but I was never invited to it.

Or what about a symposium on any of the other massacres of Indians that have taken place in American history? American history is full of them. Have you ever seen a documentary on the Civil War in which they talked about an Indian massacre? No. Whenever the Civil War is discussed, it is discussed in terms of battles between the North and the South, it's discussed in terms of other issues, including slavery. But important facts are being left out of the history of the Civil War period, one of them being that more land was taken from the Indians during the Civil War than in any other comparable period in American history. Most histories of the Civil War ignore the fact that while Union soldiers were fighting the Confederacy in the South, there were other parts of the Union army out West taking land from the Indians. In 1864 a detachment of army soldiers led by Colonel Shippington, who was also a minister, led a detachment of soldiers to Sand Creek, Colorado, and they massacred several hundred Indians. These massacres of Indians went on and on in American history.

If you look at the history of massacres in the United States, you also have to look at the massacres of black people in this country and ask whether there have been symposia on the massacre that took place in East St. Louis, Illinois, in 1917. In 1917 black people came up from the South into East St. Louis. Immigration had been cut down during the war, there was a greater demand for workers, and black people moved into East St. Louis. There were conflicts over work, over jobs, between blacks and whites in East St. Louis, and the whites went on a rampage. Several hundred black people were killed in East St. Louis in just a few days. W. E. B. Du Bois wrote an article about it in *The Crisis*, and Josephine Baker at that time took note of it and said, "The very idea of America makes me shake and tremble and gives me nightmares."

And then there were the labor massacres. I just met Dottie Engler, and I found out she's from Trinidad. "Trinidad," I said. "Wow." Not Trinidad in the West Indies, but Trinidad, Colorado. Trinidad was the site of one of the great labor struggles in American history, the Colorado Fuel and Iron Strike of 1913–1914. This strike against the Rockefeller-owned coal mines in southern Colorado was carried out for many, many months over the winter by ten to twelve thousand miners who were living in tents set up by the United Mineworkers Union and fighting off National Guard machine-gun attacks. The strike finally ended when the mine owners, the National Guard, and Rockefeller were desperate to end it. They sent two detachments of the National Guard up on a hill above the tent colony at Ludlow, Colorado, near Trinidad, and they began firing machine guns into the tents. Then they went down and set the tents on fire. The next day they found under one of the tents the bodies of eleven children and two women. And that became known as the Ludlow Massacre. Massacres of workers have taken place again and again. In Lattimer, Pennsylvania, in 1897, striking coal miners marching on a highway were shot, most in the back, by the local sheriff and his deputies, and nineteen died. In 1937, during the Republic Steel Strike, strikers moving away from the police, trying to get away, were shot in the back.

And we're not even talking now about massacres overseas—that's always the last thing we consider, what we do to people overseas. Most people know about the My Lai Massacre in Vietnam. But to my astonishment, or maybe I shouldn't have been astonished—when I talked to a group of two honors history classes in a high school recently and I asked, "How many of you here have heard of the My Lai Massacre?" not one hand was raised. It made me wonder what is being taught in schools about the war in Vietnam. But while most people know about the Ludlow Massacre, how many people know about the Moro Massacre? And how many people even know about the war in the Philippines? Because when you study history, you learn about the Spanish-American War, that "splendid little war," as they call it, a short war with very few American casualties—the perfect war. Remember, we had one like that recently, but we don't ask how many casualties there were on the other side, we never ask that question. I remember the press talked to Colin Powell at the end of the Gulf War, and he said we had had very few, virtually no, American casualties; and they asked about Iraqi casualties, and Colin Powell said, "That's none of our concern." To me, that was a deadly reiteration of what has happened all through American history. After the war with Spain, we went to war in the Philippines in 1899 to take over the Philippines. That wasn't a "splendid little war," that was a long, bloody war in which the Filipinos who wanted to run their own country were massacred by Americans. And in 1906 the Moro Massacre took place, during which a detachment of the U.S. Army poured rifle fire down into a village of six hundred men, women, and children who had no modern weapons and annihilated them all. And then these soldiers were congratulated by Theodore Roosevelt for a military victory. You may wonder why my heroes are not other people's heroes. Theodore Roosevelt usually ranks high on people's lists of the "Best Presidents." Somehow, Theodore Roosevelt is up there, even though he was a racist, a lover of war, and an imperialist. Mark Twain, who was against the annexation of the Philippines and against the war in the Philippines, spoke out bitterly against Theodore Roosevelt at the time.

So doing history is all a matter of selection and deciding what is important; and you decide what is important, really, on the basis of your present concerns. And so when I was studying history, I knew what was important to me— my growing up in a sort working-class family and my working in a shipyard made me, you might say, class conscious. I have a chapter in my memoir, *You Can't Be Neutral on a Moving Train,* called "Growing up Class-Conscious" [see chapter 7 in this volume]. My early life gave me a kind of consciousness about what is generally accepted as a wonderful American economic system—the United States being the most prosperous nation in the world and all of that. But to me it was much more complicated than that, because there were the rich and there were the poor and then there were all these people who worked hard, like my father and my mother, and had nothing to show for it. So from that point on, whenever anybody said to me (and I remember some of my students at Boston University, whose parents were successful businessmen and professionals, said this), "If you work hard in this country, you will make it," I knew this wasn't true. I knew that not all the people who worked very, very hard in this country made it. And then I looked at the people who were very wealthy and prosperous, and sometimes it seemed to me that they didn't work very hard. I didn't see any necessary relationship between how hard people worked and what their rewards were, or certainly no relationship between what contribution they made to society and what their rewards were. Nothing like that.

So I grew up with a consciousness about class in this supposedly classless society. In American culture there's a very, very powerful attempt to pretend that we don't have classes in our society. And they're always using language going back to the preamble of the Constitution, "We, the People of the United States, . . . establish. . . ." It wasn't "we the people" who established the Constitution; it was fifty-five white, prosperous men who established the Constitution. And there were people left out of it, people ignored by it, and the Constitution was not set up in order to benefit all of the people as one classless group but to benefit the upper classes of that time, to benefit the bond-holders and the slaveholders and the land speculators and the manufacturers. The very first program proposed by Alexander Hamilton in the very first Congress was a program that was designed to do just that, by paying off the speculators who had acquired war bonds, by establishing a tariff to help manufacturers, by taxing poor farmers, and creating a partnership between bankers and the government in a national bank.

If you're conscious of class in American society and you hear somebody say "Big government is bad" or you hear Bill Clinton state as he did in the 1996 presidential campaign that "the era of big government is over," you think, what a ridiculous statement. Have you looked at our national budget? Have you looked at our military? Have you looked at the power of the American government? Have you looked at the subsidies that it gives to corporations? The era of big government is over in what is called Aesopian language; what that really means is "We're not going to give as much to poor people as we used to." That's what that statement really meant. Because we've always had big government—this nation was founded on the idea of big government; that was what the Constitution was all about. Shays' Rebellion scared the Founding Fathers, and letters went back and forth saying, roughly, "Hey, look at Shays' Rebellion. We'd better do something or there are going to be rebellions all over the place. We've gotta have some control." So we have a constitution that sets up big government, a government that can protect slave owners from revolts, can protect manufacturers with tariffs, and can protect land speculators who were going out West from Indian attacks (these Indians foolishly thought that it was their land).

And so we had big government, and it remained big government all the way through U.S. history. Big government on behalf of the moneyed interests and corporations. All through the nineteenth century, government subsidies were the norm—100 million acres of land were given to the railroads, free. You try to get an acre of land from the government for free. Write a letter saying, "I've been reading about the big grants given to the railroads, 100 million acres—I just want one." Try it. In our time, subsidies have been given to the aircraft companies. At the end of World War II, the aircraft industry would have collapsed if it hadn't had huge subsidies from the American government. You can read the letters between Secretary of the Air Force W. Stuart Symington and the executives of Lockheed; Symington assures them that the government will not let them down, the government will take care of them. Does the government do the same thing for poor people? Less and less. So we've always had big government on behalf of the powerful. And it is only in the twentieth century that the government began to do things for the poor and for workers. In the early part of the twentieth century, some reform was beginning to be passed under the impact of the Socialist Party, the Industrial Workers of the World (IWW), and the strikes of that time. And then in the 1930s, legislation was passed on behalf of people who were in need—Social Security, unemployment insurance, subsidized housing, the Wagner Act, and so on. These legislations were all passed in the aftermath of the labor struggles and uprisings of the 1930s—the general strike in Minneapolis, the general strike in San Francisco, the Great Textile Strike in the South. And then you have Medicare and Medicaid coming as part of the upsurge of the 1960s. And now that government is helping the poor and not just the rich, the cry goes up: "Big government, we must do something about that." Here again knowledge of history comes in handy for dealing with the issues that come up every day.

I want to look at the popular idea of World War II being "the good war, the best of wars." Having served in World War II, I'm dubious about the value of war as a solution to any basic problems that the human race has, and that makes me look at the history of American foreign policy with a skeptical point of view. If we look at the other wars that the United States has fought, it really isn't hard to see what a sorry moral record we have had in the expansion of this country—in the Indian wars that enabled the conquest of this country, and in the Mexican War that enabled us to take half of Mexico. I think sometimes of the anti-immigration legislation in California—"keep the Mexicans out." It was their land, you see, and we took it, and now we must keep them out. And so my experience in war gave me a very, very strong conviction that wars solve nothing, really. It appears to solve something temporarily, you get rid of a particular manifestation of evil, but the fundamental evils remain in the world and in fact they're perpetuated by the fact that you used enormous violence in the course of doing away with this particular evil.

Another experience that had a strong effect on my thinking about history was teaching in the South, at Spelman College, my first real teaching job. I taught at Spelman, a black women's college in Atlanta, for seven years from 1956 to 1963. Du Bois had taught at Atlanta University, and Martin Luther King Jr. had gone to Morehouse, the men's college across the street from Spelman, and became involved in the civil rights movement there, working with the Student Nonviolent Coordinating Committee (SNCC), going wherever demonstrations were taking place—Albany, Georgia, Selma, Alabama, towns in Mississippi. And while working at Spelman, I began to look at history from an African American point of view, which had been lost to me. When I was a graduate student at Columbia, there was no work by W. E. B. Du Bois on my reading lists. Black writers were missing from the curriculum.

We learned about the Progressive Era in American history. The labeling of eras of history is always interesting. Do you remember the Era of Good Feeling? There was supposedly an Era of Good Feeling in the early part of the nineteenth century. I've tried to imagine what it was like. And every history textbook has a chapter on the Progressive Era. What made it progressive? Well, a number of reforms were passed during that period—the Hepburn Act, railroad legislation, the Meat Inspection Act (you notice how effective that's been) and amendments to the Constitution, including direct election of senators, the income tax, the creation of the Federal Reserve, and the creation of the Federal Trade Commission. That was the Progressive Era. Then you read a book by Rayford Logan, a black historian, and he informs you that the Progressive Era was that period of American history during which more black people were lynched than in any other period of American history. But that somehow gets lost when you give a label to a period of history, just as the Gay Nineties was one of the worst economic crises in American history. It was a time of labor struggles, the Pullman strike, the steel strike, and, of course, the time of the Spanish-American War and the war against the Philippines. Those all took place during the Gay Nineties. And then the Roaring Twenties, the Jazz Age. Whether you study this period in junior high school or at the graduate level, you are taught that the 1920s was the Age of Prosperity. You know very often what you learn on the graduate level is not very different from what you learn at the junior high school level, they just add footnotes. And so the 1920s is the Age of Prosperity. I did my doctoral dissertation on LaGuardia as a congressman in the 1920s. Before he became mayor of

New York and became famous, LaGuardia was a congress-man from East Harlem in the 1920s. I read the letters sent to LaGuardia by his constituents in East Harlem all through the Age of Prosperity. And these people in East Harlem were writing to him saying, "My husband is out of work, my kids don't have food, we can't pay the rent, they've turned off the gas." And then if you look closely, you could see this was happening all around the country. Beneath the headlines about Wall Street prospering, there was misery in a very large part of the population. It's instructive to see this kind of history because it prepares you for today's focus on the Dow Jones Industrial Average. Today many believe that if the Dow Jones average goes up, we're all better off. Everybody in the country is better off. That's the measure of the country's prosperity, where the Dow Jones average is. In that sense history prepares you to look beneath the surface and to ask "Prosperity for whom?" and to look at the population from a class point of view, to see who is benefiting and who is not.

Maybe the most important thing I learned from being in the South while I taught at Spelman and from being involved in the civil rights movement concerns democracy and the way social change takes place. Because I had learned, like almost every American learns in school, whether it's in junior high school or high school, about democracy. Obviously, the United States is a democracy, but what is a democracy? We'll show you, we'll put it on the blackboard. There are the three branches of government: the executive, the legislative, and the judicial. And there are checks and balances. And they draw the arrows back and forth. I remember sitting there, enthralled. This was *neat*, this was *democracy*. Checks and balances: you know, if the Congress does something bad, the president will stop it. If the president does something bad, the Congress will stop it. If they both do something bad, the Supreme Court will stop it. That meant that nothing bad would ever happen. But of course democracy can't be put on the blackboard. It's not a formula, it's not a constitution, it's not laws, it's not a framework, it's not a structure. Democracy is people acting on behalf of justice. And if you were in the South during the civil rights movement, you could see that the government wasn't doing anything about racial segregation. And I'm not just talking about the southern governments, I'm talking about the federal government, the liberal federal government of Kennedy and Johnson—they weren't doing anything about racial segregation. And the Constitution wasn't helping blacks, and Supreme Court decisions weren't being enforced. And so black people had to go out in the streets, and they had to demonstrate, and they had to get arrested, and they had to get beaten, and some of them had to get killed, and they had to take *risks*—risk their lives and their jobs, risk being thrown off the plantation, which is what happened to Fannie Lou Hamer when she tried to register to vote in Louisville, Mississippi, in 1962. And only then, only when a great commotion took place in the country, and only when that commotion had reverberated around the world, only then did the Congress begin to act and the president begin to act. And of course when you look back in American history, that's always when democracies have come alive. The great injustices that have existed in the United States were never ameliorated from the top. The eight-hour day was not legislated by Congress, it was not ordained by the Supreme Court, there was nothing in the Constitution about people's rights to work less than sixteen hours a day or fewer than seven days a week. No economic rights are guaranteed in the Constitution, except the rights of capital—

the right that "no state shall impair the obligation of contract." But economic rights for ordinary people? Or the right to health? No. People had to struggle for that; workers had to go out on strike, there had to be labor turmoil throughout the history of this country in order for workers to achieve even the eight-hour day. And that was democracy coming alive.

And so the 1960s and the civil rights movement, the antiwar movement, the women's movement, the gay movement, the disabled persons movement—that was democracy coming alive. Today we're facing a situation where all attention is focused on government—on what the president is doing, and what Congress is doing, and what the courts are doing. And that kind of focus, which is also repeated in the media again and again, drives home to the American people the idea that we are passive, that the making of history is not up to us, that it's all up to those people in Washington. That's the focus of attention. They ignore what people are doing in towns and cities all over the country. And people are doing lots of things: people are protesting, and people are trying to accomplish something, and people are trying to change things, but they don't make the national news. Poor people will stage a sit-in at the State House in Massachusetts, and they will hardly be noticed. Indians will protest against Thanksgiving Day, and they will be in the headlines one day and then they're gone. Strikes will take place all over the country, and they will not even be recorded in the press or on television. And so what we need today is a new movement. We know there are serious problems in our country; we know that we are bombing Iraq every day, and it's just a little blip in the news; and people in this country are suffering every day; and people in Massachusetts and soon in other states are having the benefits on which they depend to take care of their immediate needs, such as health care, taken away from them—that's happening every day; and there's an enormous amount of money being spent for military apparatus while education and health are suffering for lack of resources. There are serious things going on that need to be rectified. And there are movements, little movements all over the country, but what is required is for more and more people to become more active, to realize that democracy depends on us and to realize that the future of our society, as well as the lives of people abroad, depends on us and on what we do—even on the very little, little things that we do. Because the little things that people do multiply and connect at some point in history at a point that you can't even predict. And then important changes take place. That's what I get from history.

4
HOW FREE IS HIGHER EDUCATION?

⊕

Education has always inspired fear among those who want to keep the existing distributions of power and wealth as they are.

In my thirty years of teaching—in a small southern college, in a large northeastern university—I have often observed that fear. And I think I understand what it is based on. The educational environment is unique in our society: It is the only situation where an adult, looked up to as a mentor, is alone with a group of young people for a protracted and officially sanctioned period of time and can assign whatever reading he or she chooses and discuss with these young people any subject under the sun. The subject may be defined by the curriculum, by the catalog course description, but this is a minor impediment to a bold and imaginative teacher, especially in literature, philosophy, and the social sciences, where there are unlimited possibilities for free discussion of social and political issues.

This essay originally appeared as chapter 9 in *The Zinn Reader: Writings on Disobedience and Democracy* (New York: Seven Stories Press, 1997). Reprinted with minor changes by permission of the author and publisher.

That would seem to be an educational idea, an arena for free discussion, assuming a diversity of viewpoints from a variety of teachers, of the most important issues of our time. Yet it is precisely that situation in the classrooms of higher education that frightens the guardians of the status quo. They declare their admiration for such freedom in principle and suggest that radicals are insufficiently grateful for its existence. But when teachers actually *use* this freedom, introducing new subjects, new readings, and outrageous ideas, challenging authority, criticizing "Western civilization," or amending the "canon" of great books as listed by certain educational authorities of the past, then the self-appointed guardians of "high culture" become enraged.

Early in my teaching career I decided that I would make the most of the special freedom that is possible in a classroom. I would introduce what I felt to be the most important, and therefore the most controversial, questions in my class. When I was assigned, as a young professor at Spelman College, a college for black women in Atlanta, a course called "Constitutional Law," I changed the course title to "Civil Liberties" and departed from the canonized recital of Supreme Court cases. I did not ignore the most important of these cases, but I also talked with the students about social movements for justice and asked what role these movements played in changing the environment within which the Supreme Court decisions were made.

When I taught American history, I ignored the canon of the traditional textbook, in which the heroic figures were mostly presidents, generals, and industrialists. In those texts, wars were treated as problems in military strategy and not in morality; Christopher Columbus, Andrew Jackson, and Theodore Roosevelt were treated as heroes in the march of democracy, with not a word from the objects of their violence. I suggested that we approach Columbus and Jackson from the perspective of their victims, that we look at the magnificent feat of the transcontinental railroad from the viewpoint of the Irish and Chinese laborers who, in building it, died by the thousands.

Was I committing that terrible sin that is arousing the anger of today's fundamentalists: "politicizing the curriculum"? Is there any rendition of constitutional law, any recounting of American history that can escape being political—that is, expressing a political point of view? Is treating Theodore Roosevelt as a hero (which is usually done not overtly but in an expression of quiet admiration) less "political" than pointing to his role as an early imperialist, a forerunner of a long string of crude U.S. interventions in the Caribbean?

I have no doubt that I was taking a political stand when, in the early 1960s, I expressed respect for my students who missed classes to demonstrate in downtown Atlanta against racial segregation. In doing that, was I being more political than the fundamentalist Allan Bloom, at Cornell, who pointed with pride to the fact that the students in his seminar on Plato and Aristotle stuck to their studies and refused to participate in the social conflict outside the seminar room?

In my teaching I never concealed my political views: my detestation of war and militarism, my anger at radical inequality, my belief in a democratic socialism and in a rational and just distribution of world's wealth. To pretend to an "objectivity" that was neither possible nor desirable seemed to me dishonest. I made it clear to my students at the start of each course that they would be getting *my* point of view on the subjects under discussion, that I would try to be fair to other points of view, that I would scrupulously uphold their right to disagree with me. My students had a long experience of political indoctrination before they arrived in my class—in the family, in high school, in movies and television. They would hear viewpoints other than mine in other courses and for the rest of their lives. I insisted on my right to enter my opinions in the marketplace of ideas, so long dominated by orthodoxy.

Surely the expression of "political views" (what is just, or unjust? what can citizens do?) is inevitable in education. It may be done overtly, honestly, or it may be there subtly. But it is always there, however the textbook, by its very bulk and dullness, pretends to neutrality, however noncommittal is the teacher. It is inevitably there because all education involves *selection*—of events, of voices, of books—and any insistence on one list of great books or great figures or great events is a partial (in both senses of that term) rendering of our cultural heritage.

Therefore it seems to me that the existence of free expression in higher education must mean the opportunity for many points of view, many political biases, to be presented to students. This requires a true pluralism of readings, ideas, viewpoints—a genuinely free marketplace of thought and culture. Let both Shakespeare and Wole Soyinka, Bach and Leonard Bernstein, Dickens and W. E. B. Du Bois, John Stuart Mill and Zora Neale Hurston, Rembrandt and Picasso, Plato and Lao-tzu, Locke and Marx, Aeschylus and August Wilson, Jane Austen and Gabriel Garcia Márquez be available to students.

Such a free marketplace of ideas does not depend essentially on "the curriculum." How many words have been wasted moving those empty shells around the debating table! What is crucial is the content of those shells, which depends on who the teachers are and who the students are. A thoughtful teacher can take a course titled "Western Civilization" and enlarge its content with an exciting global perspective. Another teacher can be given a course grandly called "World Civilization" and give the student an eclectic, limp recounting of dull events and meaningless dates.

The pluralism in thought that is required for truly free expression in higher education has never been realized. Its crucial elements—an ideologically diverse faculty, a hetero-geneous student body (in class, race, sex—words that bring moans from the keepers of the "higher culture")—have always been under attack from outside and from inside the colleges and universities.

McCarthyism, in which the corporate nature of academ-ic institutions revealed itself in the surrender of university administrators to government inquisitors (see Ellen Schreck-er's book *No Ivory Tower: McCarthyism in the Universities* for the details), was only the most flagrant of the attacks on freedom of expression. More subtle, more persistent, has been the control of faculty appointments, contract re-newals, and tenure (inevitably with political considerations) by colleagues, but especially by administrators, who are the universities' links with the dominant forces of American society—the government, the corporations, the military.

Boston University, where I taught for many years, is not too far from typical, with its panoply of military and gov-ernment connections—ROTC chapters for military service, former government officials given special faculty posts, the board of trustees dominated by corporate executives, a president eager to curry favor with powerful politicos. Al-most all colleges and universities are organized as admin-istrative hierarchies in which a president and trustees, usually well connected to wealthy and important people in the outside world, make the critical decisions as to who may enjoy the freedom of the classroom to speak to the young people of the new generation.

Higher education, while enjoying some special privileges, is still part of the American system, which is an ingenious, sophisticated system of control. It is not totalitarian; what permits it to be called a democracy is that it allows apertures of liberty on the supposition that this will not endanger the basic contours of wealth and power in the society. It trusts that the very flexibility of a partially free system will assure its survival, even contribute to its strength. Our government is so confident of its power that it can risk allowing some political choice to the people, who can vote for Democrats or Republicans but find huge obstacles of money and bureaucracy if they want an alternative. Our corporations are so wealthy that they can afford some distribution of wealth to a supportive middle class, but not to the thirty or forty million people who live in the cellars of society. The system can allow special space for free expression in its cultural institutions: the theater, the arts, the media. But the size of that space is controlled by money and power; the profit motive limits what is put on stage or screen; government officials dominate the informational role of the news media.

Yes, there is, indeed, a special freedom of expression in the academy. How can I at Boston University, or Noam Chomsky at MIT, or David Montgomery at Yale deny that we have had more freedom in the university than we would have had in business or other professions? But those who tolerate us know that our numbers are few, that our students, however excited by new ideas, go out into a world of economic pressures and exhortations to caution. And they know too that they can point to us as an example of the academy's openness to all ideas. True, there is a tradition of academic freedom, but it is based on a peculiar unspoken contract. The student, in return for the economic security of a career and several years with some degree of free intellectual play, is expected upon graduation to become an obedient citizen, participating happily in the nation's limited pluralism (be a Republican or a Democrat, but please, nothing else).

The boundaries for free expression in the university, though broader than in the larger society, are still watched carefully. When that freedom is used, even by a small minority, to support social change considered dangerous by the guardians of the status quo, the alarm goes out: "The communists are infiltrating our institutions"; "Marxists have taken over the curriculum"; "feminists and black militants are destroying classical education." Their reaction approaches hysteria: "With a few notable exceptions, our most prestigious liberal arts colleges and universities have installed the entire radical menu at the center of their humanities curriculum," says Roger Kimball in his book *Tenured Radicals*. The shrillness of such alarms is never proportionate to the size of the radical threat. But the Establishment takes no chances. Thus J. Edgar Hoover and Joseph McCarthy saw imminent danger of communist control of the U.S. government; protectors of "the canon" see "tenured radicals" taking over higher education. The axes then get sharpened.

Yes, some of us radicals have somehow managed to get tenure. But far from dominating higher education, we remain a carefully watched minority. Some of us may continue to speak and write and teach as we like, but we have seen the ax fall countless times on colleagues less lucky. And who can deny the chilling effect this has had on other faculty, with or without tenure, who have censored themselves rather than risk a loss of promotion, a lower salary, a nonrenewal of contract, or a denial of tenure?

Perhaps, after all, Boston University cannot be considered typical, having had for twenty years probably the most authoritarian, the most politically watchful university president in the country. But although it is hard to match John Silber as an educational tyrant, he can be considered (I base this on spending some time at other universities) not a departure from the norm, but an exaggeration of it.

Have we had freedom of expression at Boston University?

A handful of radical teachers, in a faculty of over a thousand, was enough to have John Silber go into fits over our presence on campus, just as certain observers of higher education are now getting apoplectic over what they see as radical dominance nationwide. These are ludicrous fantasies, but they lead to attacks on the freedom of expression of those faculty members who manage to overcome that prudent self-control so prominent among academics. At Boston University it must have been such fantasies that led Silber to determinedly destroy the faculty union, which was a minor threat to his control over faculty. He handled appointments and tenure with the very political criteria that his conservative educational companions so loudly decry. In at least seven cases that I know of, where the candidates were politically undesirable by Silber's standards, he ignored overwhelming faculty recommendations and refused them tenure.

Did I have freedom of expression in my classroom? I did, because I followed Aldous Huxley's advice: "Liberties are not given; they are taken." But it was obviously infuriating to John Silber that every semester four hundred students signed up to take my courses, whether they were "Law and Justice in America" or "An Introduction to Political Theory." And so he did what is often done in the academy; he engaged in petty harassments—withholding salary raises, denying teaching assistants. He also threatened to fire me (and four other members of the union) when we held our classes in the street rather than cross the picket lines of striking secretaries.

The fundamentalists of politics—the Reagans, Bushes, Helmses—want to pull the strings of control tighter on the distribution of wealth, power, and civil liberties. The fundamentalists of law, the Borks and Rehnquists, want to interpret the Constitution so as to put strict limits on the legal possibilities for social reform. The fundamentalists of education fear the possibilities inherent in the unique freedom of discussion that we find in higher education. And so, under the guise of defending "the common culture" or "disinterested scholarship" or "Western civilization," they attack that freedom. They fear exactly what some of us hope for, that if students are given wider political choices in the classroom than they get in the polling booth or the workplace, they may become social rebels. They may join movements for racial or sexual equality or against war, or, even more dangerous, work for what James Madison feared as he argued for a conservative Constitution: "an equal division of property." Let us hope so.

5
COLUMBUS AND WESTERN
CIVILIZATION

✑

George Orwell, who was a very wise man, wrote: "Who controls the past controls the future. And who controls the present controls the past." In other words, those who dominate our society are in a position to write our histories. And if they can do that, they can decide our futures. That is why the telling of the Columbus story is important. Let me make a confession. I knew very little about Columbus until about twelve years ago, when I began writing my book *A People's History of the United States*. I had a Ph.D. in history from Columbia University—that is, I had the proper training of a historian—but what I knew about Columbus was pretty much what I had learned in elementary school.

But when I began to write my *People's History*, I decided I must learn about Columbus. I had already concluded that I did not want to write just another overview of American history—I knew my point of view would be

This essay was originally delivered as a lecture at the University of Wisconsin–Madison in October 1991.

different. I was going to write about the United States from the point of view of those people who had been largely neglected in the history books: the indigenous Americans, black slaves, women, and working people, whether native or immigrant.

I wanted to tell the story of the nation's industrial progress from the standpoint not of Rockefeller, Carnegie, and Vanderbilt but of the people who worked in their mines and their oil fields and those who lost their limbs or their lives building the railroads. I wanted to tell the story of wars not from the standpoint of generals and presidents, not from the standpoint of those military heroes whose statues you see all over this country, but through the eyes of the GIs or through the eyes of "the enemy." Yes, why not look at the Mexican War, that great military triumph of the United States, from the viewpoint of the Mexicans?

And so, how must I tell the story of Columbus? I concluded that I must see him through the eyes of the people who were here when he arrived, the people he called "Indians" because he thought he was in Asia. Well, they left no memoirs, no histories. Their culture was an oral culture, not a written one. Besides, they had been wiped out in a few decades after Columbus's arrival. So I was compelled to turn to the next best thing: the Spaniards who were on the scene at the time. First, Columbus himself. He had kept a journal.

Columbus's journal was revealing. He described the people who greeted him when he landed in the Bahamas—they were Arawak Indians, sometimes called Tainos—and told how they waded out into the sea to greet him and his men, who must have looked and sounded like people from another world, and brought them gifts of various kinds. Columbus described them as peaceable, gentle, and said: "They do not bear arms, and do not know for I showed them a sword—they took it by the edge and cut themselves."

Throughout his journal, over the next months, Columbus spoke of the Native Americans with what seemed like admiring awe: "They are the best people in the world and above all the gentlest—without knowledge of what is evil—nor do they murder or steal. . . . They love their neighbors as themselves and they have the sweetest talk in the world . . . always laughing."

And in a letter he wrote to one of his Spanish patrons, Columbus said, "They are very simple and honest and exceedingly liberal with all they have." In his journal, Columbus writes: "They would make fine servants. With fifty men we could subjugate them all and make them do whatever we want." Yes, this was how Columbus saw the Indians—not as hospitable hosts but as servants, to "do whatever we want."

And what did Columbus want? This is not hard to determine. In the first two weeks of journal entries, there is one word that recurs seventy-five times: *gold*. In the standard accounts of Columbus, what is emphasized again and again is his religious feeling, his desire to convert the natives to Christianity, his reverence for the Bible. Yes, he was concerned about God. But he was more concerned about gold. Just one additional letter; his was a limited alphabet. All over the islands of Hispaniola, where Columbus, his brothers, and his men spent most of their time, he erected crosses. But they also built gallows all over the island—340 of them by the year 1500. Crosses and gallows—that deadly historic juxtaposition.

In his quest for gold, Columbus, seeing bits of gold among the Indians, concluded there were huge amounts of it. He ordered the natives to find a certain amount of gold within a certain period of time. And if they did not meet their quota, their arms were hacked off. The others were supposed to learn from this and deliver the gold. Samuel Eliot Morison, the Harvard historian who was Columbus's admiring biographer, acknowledged this. He wrote, "Whoever thought up this ghastly system, Columbus was responsible for it, as the only means of producing gold for export. . . . Those who fled to the mountains were hunted with hounds, and those who escaped, starvation and disease took toll, while thousands of poor creatures in desperation took cassava poison to end their miseries." Morison continues, "So the policy and acts of Columbus for which he alone was responsible began the depopulation of the terrestrial paradise that was Hispaniola in 1492. Of the original natives, estimated by modern ethnologists at 300,000 in number, one-third were killed off between 1494 and 1496. By 1508, an enumeration showed only 60,000 alive. . . . In 1548 Oviedo [Morison is referring to Fernández de Oviedo, the official Spanish historian of conquest] doubted whether 500 Indians remained."

But Columbus could not obtain enough gold to send home to impress the king and queen and his Spanish financiers, so he decided to send back to Spain another kind of loot: slaves. They rounded up about 1,200 natives, selected 500, and sent them, jammed together, on the voyage across the Atlantic. Two hundred died on the way of cold and sickness. In Columbus's journal a September 1498 entry reads, "From here one might send, in the name of Holy Trinity, as many slaves as could be sold. . . ."

What the Spaniards did to the Indians is told in horrifying detail by Bartolomé de las Casas, whose writings give the most thorough account of the Spanish–Indian encounter. Las Casas was a Dominican priest who came to the New World a few years after Columbus, spent forty years on Hispaniola and nearby islands, and became the leading advocate in Spain for the rights of the natives. In his book *The Devastation of the Indies,* Las Casas writes of the Arawaks, "of all the infinite universe of humanity, these people are the most guileless, the most devoid of wickedness and duplicity . . . yet into this sheepfold . . . there came some Spaniards who immediately behaved like ravening beasts. . . . Their reason for killing and destroying . . . is that Christians have an ultimate aim which is to acquire gold. . . ."

The cruelties multiplied. Las Casas saw soldiers stabbing Indians for sport, dashing babies' heads on rocks. And when the Indians resisted, the Spaniards hunted them down, equipped for killing with horses, armor plate, lances, pikes, rifles, crossbows, and vicious dogs. Indians who took things belonging to Spaniards—they were not accustomed to the concept of private ownership and gave freely of their own possessions—were beheaded or burned at the stake.

Las Casas's testimony was corroborated by other eyewitnesses. A group of Dominican friars, addressing the Spanish monarchy in 1519 hoping for the Spanish government to intercede, told about unspeakable atrocities, children thrown to dogs to be devoured, newborn babies born to women prisoners flung into the jungle to die. Forced labor in the mines and on the land led to much sickness and death. Many children died because their mothers, overworked and starved, had no milk for them. Las Casas estimated that in Cuba seven thousand children died in three months.

The greatest toll was taken by sickness, because the Europeans brought with them diseases against which the natives had no immunity: typhoid, typhus, diphtheria, smallpox. And, as in any military conquest, women came in for especially brutal treatment. One Italian nobleman named Cueno recorded an early sexual encounter. The "admiral" he refers to is Columbus, who, as part of his agreement with the Spanish monarchy, insisted he be made an admiral. Cueno wrote, "I captured a very beautiful Carib women, whom the said Lord Admiral gave to me and with whom . . . I conceived desire to take pleasure. I wanted to put my desire into execution but she did not want it and treated me with her finger nails in such manner that I wished I had never begun. But seeing that, I took a rope and thrashed her well. . . . Finally we came to an agreement."

There is other evidence of the widespread rape of native women. According to Samuel Eliot Morison, "in the Bahamas, Cuba and Hispaniola they found young beautiful women, who everywhere were naked, in most places accessible, and presumably complaisant." Who presumes this? Morison, and so many others. Morison saw the conquest as so many writers after him have done, as one of the great romantic adventures of world history. He seemed to get carried away by what appeared to him to be a masculine conquest. He wrote, "Never again may mortal men hope to recapture the amazement, the wonder, the delight of those October days in 1492, when the new world gracefully yielded her virginity to the conquering Castilians." The language of Cueno ("we came to an agreement") and of Morison ("gracefully yield"), written almost five hundred years apart, surely suggests how persistent through modern history has been the mythology that rationalizes sexual brutality by seeing it as "complaisant."

So, I read Columbus's journal, and I read Las Casas. I also read Hans Koning's pioneering work of our time— *Columbus: His Enterprise,* which, at the time I wrote my *People's History* was the only contemporary account I could find that departed from the standard treatment.

When my book appeared, I began to get letters from all over the country about it. Here was a book of six hundred pages, starting with Columbus and ending with the 1970s, and all the letters were about one subject: Columbus. Since I discuss Columbus at the very beginning of the book, I could have interpreted this to mean that that's all these people had read. But no, it seemed that the Columbus story was simply the part of my book that readers found most startling. Because every American, from elementary school on, learns the Columbus story and learns it the same way: "In fourteen hundred and ninety-two, Columbus sailed the ocean blue."

How many of you have heard of Tigard, Oregon? Well, I hadn't until, about seven years ago, I began receiving twenty or thirty letters every semester from students at a high school in Tigard, Oregon. It seems that their teacher was having them (knowing high schools, I almost said "forcing them to") read my *People's History*. He was photocopying a number of the chapters and giving them to the students. And then he had them write letters to me with comments and questions. Roughly half of them thanked me for giving them data that they had never seen before. The others were angry or wondered how I had gotten such information and how I had arrived at such outrageous conclusions. One high school student named Bethany wrote, "Out of all the articles that I've read of yours I found 'Columbus, the Indians, and Human Progress' the most shocking." Another student named Brian, seventeen years old, wrote, "An example of the confusion I feel after reading your article concerns Columbus coming to America. . . . According to you, it seems he came for women, slaves, and gold. You've said you have gained a lot of this information from Columbus' own journal. I am wondering if there is such a journal, and if so, why isn't it part of our history. Why isn't any of what you say in my history book, or in history books people have access to each day." I pondered this letter. It could be interpreted to mean that the writer was indignant that no other history books had told him what I did. Or, more likely, he was saying. "I don't believe a word of what you wrote! You made this up!"

I am not surprised at such reactions. It tells something about the claims of pluralism and diversity in American culture, the pride in our "free society," that generation after generation has learned exactly the same set of facts about Columbus and finished their education with the same glaring omissions.

A schoolteacher in Portland, Oregon, named Bill Bigelow has undertaken a crusade to change the way the Columbus story is taught all over America. He tells of how he sometimes starts a new class. He goes over to a girl in the front row and takes her purse. She says, "You took my purse!" Bigelow responds, "No, I discovered it." Bill Bigelow did a study of recent children's books on Columbus. He found them remarkably alike in their repetition of the traditional point of view. A typical fifth-grade biography of Columbus begins, "There once was a boy who loved the salty sea." Well! I can imagine a children's biography of Attila the Hun beginning with the sentence "There once was a boy who loved horses." Another children's book in Bigelow's study, this time for second-graders, begins, "The king and queen looked at the gold and the Indians. They listened in wonder to Columbus' stories of adventure. Then they all went to church to pray and sing. Tears of joy filled Columbus' eyes."

I once spoke about Columbus to a workshop of schoolteachers, and one of them suggested that schoolchildren were too young to hear of the horrors recounted by Las

Casas and others. Others disagreed, said children's stories include plenty of violence, but the perpetrators are witches and monsters and "bad people," not national heroes who have holidays named after them. Some of the teachers made suggestions on how the truth could be told in a way that would not frighten children unnecessarily but that would avoid the falsification of history. The argument about children not being ready to hear the truth does not account for the fact that, in American society, when the children grow up they are still not told the truth. As I said earlier, right up through graduate school I was not presented with the information that would counter the myths told to me in the early grades. And it is clear that my experience is typical, judging from the shocked reactions to my book that I have received from readers of all ages.

If you look in an adult book, the *Columbus Encyclopedia* (my edition was put together in 1950, but all the relevant information was available then, including Morison's biography), there is a long entry on Columbus (about one thousand words) but you find no mention of the atrocities committed by him and his men. In the 1986 edition of the *Columbia History of the World,* there are several mentions of Columbus, but nothing about what he did to the natives. Several pages are devoted to "Spain and Portugal in America," in which the treatment of the native population is presented as a matter of controversy among the theologians at the time and among historians today. You can get the flavor of this "balanced approach," containing a nugget of reality, by the following passage from that history. "The determination of the Crown and the Church to Christianize the Indians, the need for labor to exploit the new lands, and the attempts of some Spaniards to protect the Indians, resulted in a very remarkable complex of customs, laws, and institutions which even today leads historians to contradictory conclusions about Spanish rule in America. . . . Academic disputes flourish on this debatable and in a sense insoluble question, but there is no doubt that cruelty, overwork and disease resulted in an appalling depopulation. There were, according to recent estimates, about 25 million Indians in Mexico in 1519, slightly more than 1 million in 1605." Despite this scholarly language— "contradictory conclusions . . . academic disputes . . . insoluble question"—there is no real dispute about the facts of enslavement, forced labor, rape, murder, the taking of hostages, the ravages of disease carried from Europe, and the wiping out of huge numbers of native people. The only dispute is over how much emphasis is to be placed on these facts and how they carry over into the issues of our time.

For instance, Samuel Eliot Morison does spend some time detailing the treatment of the natives by Columbus and his men and uses the word "genocide" to describe the overall effect of the "discovery." But he buries this in the midst of a long, admiring treatment of Columbus, and he sums up his view in the concluding paragraphs of his popular book *Christopher Columbus, Mariner* as follows: "He had his faults and his defects, but they were largely the defects of the qualities that made him great—his indomitable will, his superb faith in God and in his own mission as the Christ-bearer to lands beyond the seas, his stubborn persistence despite neglect, poverty and discouragement. But there was no flaw, no dark side to the most outstanding and essential of all his qualities—his seamanship." Yes, his seamanship!

Let me make myself clear. I am not interested in either denouncing or exalting Columbus. It is too late for that. We are not writing a letter of recommendation for him to decide his qualifications for undertaking another voyage to another part of the universe. To me, the Columbus story is important for what it tells us about ourselves, about our time, about the decisions we make for our country and for the next century.

Why this great controversy today about Columbus and the celebration of the quincentennial? Why the indignation of Native Americans and others about the glorification of that conqueror? Why the heated defense of Columbus by others? The intensity of the debate can only be because it is not about 1492 but about 1992.

We can get a clue to this if we look back a hundred years to 1892, the year of the quadricentennial. There were great celebrations in Chicago and New York. In New York there were five days of parades, fireworks, military marches, and naval pageants, a million visitors to the city, and a memorial statue unveiled at a corner of Central Park, now to be known as Columbus Circle. A celebratory meeting took place at Carnegie Hall, addressed by Chauncey Depew.

You might not know the name of Chauncey Depew unless you recently looked at Gustavus Myers's classic work, *A History of the Great American Fortune.* In that book, Chauncey Depew is described as the front man for Cornelius Vanderbilt and his New York Central Railroad. Depew traveled to Albany, the capital of New York State, with satchels of money and free railroad passes for members of the New York State Legislature, and he came away with subsidies and land grants for the New York Central. Depew saw the Columbus festivities as a celebration of wealth and prosperity—you might say it "marks the wealth and the civilization of a great people . . . it marks the things that belong to their comfort and their ease, their pleasure and their luxuries . . . and their power." We might know that at the time he said this, there was much suffering among the working poor of America huddled in the city slums, their children sick and undernourished. The plight of people who worked on the land—which at this time was a considerable part of the population—was desperate, leading to the anger of the Farmers' Alliances and the rise of the People's (Populist) Party. And the following year, 1893, was a year of economic crisis and widespread misery.

Depew must have sensed, as he stood on the platform at Carnegie Hall, some murmurings of discontent at the smugness that accompanied that spirit of historical inquiry that doubts everything, that modern spirit that destroys all the illusions and all the heroes that have been the inspirations of patriotism through all the centuries. So, to celebrate Columbus was to be patriotic. To doubt was to be unpatriotic. And what did "patriotism" mean to Depew? It meant the glorification of expansion and conquest—which Columbus represented, and which America represented. It was just six years after his speech that the United States, expelling Spain from Cuba, began its own long occupation (sporadically military, continuously political and economic) of Cuba, took Puerto Rico and Hawaii, and began its bloody war against the Filipinos to take over their country.

That "patriotism" that was tied to the celebration of Columbus and the celebration of conquest was reinforced in the Second World War by the emergence of the United States as the superpower, with all the old European empires now in decline. At that time, Henry Luce, the powerful president-maker and multimillionaire, owner of *Time, Life,* and *Fortune* (not just the publications, but the things!), wrote that the twentieth century was turning into the "American Century," in which the United States would have its way in the world.

George H. W. Bush, accepting the presidential nomination in 1988, said: "This has been called the American

Century because in it we were the dominant force of good in the world. . . . Now we are on the verge of a new century, and what country's name will it bear? I say it will be another American Century."

What arrogance, that the twenty-first century should already be anticipated as an American century, or as any one nation's century, when we should be getting away from the murderous jingoism of the twentieth century. Bush must have thought of himself as a new Columbus, "discovering" and planting his nation's flag on a new world, because he called for a U.S. colony on the moon early in the next century and forecast a mission to Mars in the year 2019.

The "patriotism" that Chauncey Depew invoked in celebrating Columbus was profoundly tied to the notion of the inferiority of the conquered peoples. Columbus's attacks on the Indians were justified by their status as subhumans. The taking of Texas and much of Mexico by the United States just before the Civil War was done with the same racist rationale. Sam Houston, the first governor of Texas, proclaimed, "The Anglo-Saxon race must pervade the whole southern extremity of this vast continent. The Mexicans are no better than the Indians and I see no reasons why we should not take their land."

At the start of the twentieth century, the violence of the new American expansionism into the Caribbean and the Pacific was accepted because we were dealing with lesser beings. In the year 1900, Chauncey Depew, now a U.S. senator, spoke again in Carnegie Hall, this time to support Theodore Roosevelt's candidacy for vice president. Celebrating the conquest of the Philippines as the beginning of the American penetration of China and more, he proclaimed, "The guns of Dewey in Manila Bay were heard across Asia and Africa, they echoed through the palace at

Peking and brought to the Oriental mind a new potent force among western nations. We, in common with the countries of Europe, are striving to enter the limitless markets of the east. . . . These people respect nothing but power. I believe the Philippines will be enormous markets and sources of wealth." Theodore Roosevelt, who appears endlessly on lists of our "great presidents" and whose face is one of the four colossal sculptures of American presidents (along with Washington, Jefferson, and Lincoln) carved into Mount Rushmore in South Dakota, called the failure to annex Hawaii in 1893 "a crime against white civilization."

In his book *The Strenuous Life*, Roosevelt wrote, "Of course our whole national history has been one of expansion. . . . That the barbarians recede or are conquered . . . is due solely to the power of the mighty civilized races which have not lost the fighting instinct." An army officer in the Philippines put it even more bluntly: "There is no use mincing words. . . . We exterminated the American Indians and I guess most of us are proud of it . . . and we must have no scruples about extermination this other race standing in the way of progress and enlightenment, if it is necessary. . . ."

The official historian of the Indies in the early sixteenth century, Fernández de Oviedo, did not deny what was done to natives by the conquistadors. He described "innumerable cruel deaths as countless as the stars." But this was acceptable, because "to use gunpowder against pagans is to offer incense to the Lord." (One is reminded of President McKinley's decision to send the army and navy to take the Philippines, saying it was the duty of the United States to "Christianize and civilize" the Filipinos.) And against Las Casas's pleas for mercy to the Indians, the theologian Juan Ginés de Sepúlveda declared, "How can we doubt that these people, so uncivilized, so barbaric, so contaminated with so many sins and obscenities, have been justly conquered."

In the year 1531, Sepúlveda visited his former college in Spain and was outraged by the students there protesting Spain's war against Turkey. The students were saying, "All war . . . is [in] contrast to the Catholic religion." This led him to write a philosophical defense of the Spanish treatment of the Indians. He quoted Aristotle, who wrote in his *Politics* that some people were "slaves by nature" who "would be hunted down like wild beasts in order to bring them to the correct way of life." Las Casas responded, "Let us send Aristotle packing, for we have in our favor the command of Christ: Thou shalt love thy neighbor as thyself."

The dehumanization of the "enemy" has been a necessary accompaniment to wars of conquest. It is easier to explain atrocities if they are committed against infidels or people of an inferior race. Slavery and racial segregation in the United States and European imperialism in Asia and Africa were justified in this way. The U.S. bombings of Vietnamese villages, the search and destroy missions, and the My Lai Massacre were all made palatable to their perpetrators by the idea that the victims were not human. They were "gooks" or "communists," and they deserved what they received.

In the Gulf War, the dehumanization of the Iraqis consisted of not recognizing their existence. We were not bombing women and children, not bombing and shelling ordinary Iraqi young men in the act of flight and surrender. We were acting against a Hitler-like monster, Saddam Hussein, although the people we were killing were the Iraqi victims of this monster. When General Colin Powell was asked about Iraqi causalities, he said that was "really not a matter I am terribly interested in." The American people were led to accept the violence of the war in Iraq because the Iraqis were made invisible—because the United States only used "smart bombs." The major media ignored the enormous death toll in Iraq, ignored the report of the Harvard medical team that visited Iraq shortly after the war and found that tens of thousands of Iraqi children were dying because of the bombing of the water supply and the resultant epidemic of disease.

The celebrations of Columbus are declared to be celebrations not just of his maritime exploits but of "progress," of his arrival in the Bahamas at the beginning of that much-praised five hundred years of "Western civilization." But those concepts need to be reexamined. When Gandhi was once asked what he though about Western civilization, he replied: "It's a good idea." The point is not to deny the benefits of "progress" and "civilization"—advances in technology, knowledge, science, health, education, and standards of living. But there is a question to be asked: Progress, yes, but at what human cost? Is progress simply to be measured in the statistics of industrial and technological change, without regard to the consequences of that "progress" for human beings? Would we accept a Russian justification of Stalin's rule, including the enormous toll in human suffering, on the grounds that he made Russia a great industrial power?

I recall that when my high school American history classes came to the period after the Civil War, roughly the years between that war and World War I, it was looked on as the Gilded Age, the period of the great Industrial Revolution, when the United States became an economic giant. I remember how thrilled we were to learn of the dramatic growth of the steel and oil industries, of the building of the great fortunes, of the crisscrossing of the country by the railroads. We were not told of the human cost of this great industrial progress: how the huge production of cotton came from the labor of black slaves; how the textile industry was built up by the labor of young girls who began work at the mills at age twelve and died at twenty-five; how the railroads were constructed by Irish and Chinese immigrants who were literally worked to death in the heat of summer and cold of winter; how working people, immigrants and native born, had to go out on strike to win the eight-hour day; how the children of the working class, in the slums of the city, had to drink polluted water, and how they died early of malnutrition and disease. All this was in the name of "progress."

And yes, there are huge benefits from industrialization, science, technology, and medicine. But so far, in these five hundred years of Western civilization, of Western domination of the rest of the world, most of those benefits have gone to a small part of the human race. Billions of people in the third world still face starvation, homelessness, disease, and the early deaths of their children.

Did the Columbus expedition mark the transition from savagery to civilization? What of the Indian civilizations that had been built up over thousands of years before Columbus came? Las Casas and others marveled at the spirit of sharing and generosity that marked the Indians societies, the communal building in which they lived, their aesthetic sensibilities, the egalitarianism among men and women. The British colonists in North America were startled at the democracy of the Iroquois—the tribes that occupied much of New York and Pennsylvania. American historian Gary Nash described Iroquois culture: "No laws and ordinances, sheriffs and constables, judges and juries, or courts or jails—the apparatus of authority in European societies—were to be found in the northeast woodlands prior to European arrival. Yet boundaries of acceptable behavior were firmly set. Through priding themselves on the autonomous individual, the Iroquois maintained a strict sense of right and wrong. . . ."

In the course of westward expansion, the new nation, the United States, stole the Indians' land, killed them when they resisted, destroyed their sources of food and shelter, pushed them into smaller and smaller sections of the country, and went about the systematic destruction of Indian society. At the time of the Black Hawk War in the 1830s—one of hundreds of wars waged against the Indians of North America— Lewis Cass, the governor of the Michigan territory, referred to his taking of millions of acres from the Indians as "the progress of civilization." He said: "A barbarous people cannot live in contact with a civilized community."

We get the sense of how "barbarous" these Indians were when we look at the 1880s, when Congress prepared legislation to break up the communal lands in which the Indians still lived into small, private possessions, what some people today would call admiringly "privatization." Senator Henry Dawes, author of this legislation, visited the Cherokee Nation, and described what he found: "there was not a family in the whole nation that had not a home of its own. There was not a pauper in the nation, and the nation did not owe a dollar. . . . It built its own schools and its hospitals. Yet the defect of the system was apparent. They have got as far as they can go, because they own their land in common. . . . There is not enterprise to make your home any better than that of your neighbors. There is no selfishness, which is at the bottom of civilization."

That selfishness at the bottom of "civilization" is connected with what drove Columbus on and what is much praised today, as American political leaders and the media speak about how the West will do a great favor to the

Soviet Union and Eastern Europe by introducing "the profit motive." Granted, there may be certain ways in which the incentive of profit may be helpful in economic development, but that incentive, in the history of the "free market" in the West, has had horrendous consequences. It led, throughout the centuries of "Western civilization," to a ruthless imperialism.

In the novella *Heart of Darkness,* written in the 1890s after he had spent some time in the Upper Congo of Africa, Joseph Conrad describes the work done by black men in chains on behalf of white men who were interested only in ivory. He writes, "The word 'ivory' rang in the air, was whispered, was sighed. You would think they were praying to it. . . . To tear treasure out of the bowels of the land was their desire, with no more moral purpose at the back of it than there is in burglars breaking into a safe." The uncontrolled drive for profit has led to enormous human suffering, exploitation, slavery, cruelty in the workplace, dangerous working conditions, child labor, the destruction of land and forests, and the poisoning of the air we breath, the water we drink, and the food we eat. In his 1933 autobiography, Chief Luther Standing Bear wrote, "True the white man brought great change. But the varied fruits of his civilization, though highly colored and inviting, are sickening and deadening. And if it be the part of civilization to maim, rob, and thwart, then what is progress? I am going to venture that the man who sat on the ground in his tipi meditating on life and its meaning, accepting the kinship of all creatures, and acknowledging unity with the universe of things, was infusing into his being the true essence of civilization."

The present threats to the environment have caused a reconsideration among scientists and other scholars of the value of "progress" as it has so far been defined. In

December 1991 there was a two-day conference at MIT in which fifty scientists and historians discussed the idea of progress in Western thought. Here is part of the report on that conference from the *Boston Globe*: "In a world where resources are being squandered and the environment poisoned, participants in a MIT conference said yesterday, it is time for people to start thinking in terms of sustainability and stability rather than growth and progress. . . . Verbal fireworks and heated exchanges that sometimes grew into shouting matches punctuated the discussions among scholars of economics, religion, medicine, history and the sciences." One of the participants, historian Leo Marx, said that working toward a more harmonious coexistence with nature is itself a kind of progress, but different than the traditional one in which people try to overpower nature.

So, to look back at Columbus in a critical way is to raise all these question about progress, civilization, our relationships with one another, and our relationship to the natural world. You probably have heard—as I have, quite often—that it is wrong for us to treat the Columbus story the way we do. What these people say is, "You are taking Columbus out of context, looking at him with the eyes of the twentieth century. You must not superimpose the values of our time on events that took place five hundred years ago. That is ahistorical." I find this argument strange. Does it mean that cruelty, exploitation, greed, enslavement, and violence against helpless people are values peculiar to the fifteenth and sixteenth centuries and that we in the twentieth century are beyond them? Are there not certain human values that are common to the age of Columbus and to our own? Proof of this is that in both his time and ours there were enslavers and exploiters; and that in both his time and ours there were those who protested against slavery and exploitation and in favor of human rights.

It is encouraging that, in this year of the quincentennial, there is a wave of protest, unprecedented in all the years of Columbus celebrations all over the United States and throughout the Americas. Much of this protest is being led by Indians, who are organizing conferences and meetings, who are engaging in acts of civil disobedience, who are trying to educate the American public about what really happened five hundred years ago and what it tells us about the issues of our time.

It is also encouraging that there is a new generation of teachers in our schools and that many of them are insisting that the Columbus story be told from the point of view of the Native Americans. In the fall of 1990 I was telephoned by a talk-show host from Los Angeles who wanted to discuss Columbus. Also on the line was a high school student from that city, named Blake Lindsey, who had insisted on addressing the Los Angeles City council to oppose the traditional Columbus Day celebrations. She told them of the genocide committed by the Spaniards against the Arawak Indians. The city council did not respond. Someone called in on that talk show, introducing herself as a woman who had emigrated from Haiti. She said, "That girl is right—we have no Indians left—in our last uprising against government the people knocked down the statue of Columbus and now it is in the basement of the city hall in Port-au-Prince." The caller finished by saying, "Why don't we build statues for the aborigines?"

Despite the misleading textbooks still in use, more teachers are questioning, and more students are questioning. Bill Bigelow reports on the reactions of his students after he introduces them to reading material that contradicts the traditional histories. One student wrote, "In 1492, Columbus sailed the ocean blue. . . . That story is about as complete as Swiss cheese." Another wrote a critique of her American history textbook to its publisher, Allyn and Bacon, pointing to many important omissions in that text. She wrote, "I'll just pick one topic to keep it simple. How about Columbus?" Another student wrote, "It seemed to me as if the publishers had just printed up some glory story that was supposed to make us feel more patriotic about our country. . . . They want us to look at our country as great and powerful and forever right. . . . We're being fed lies." When students discover that in the very first history they learn—the story of Columbus—they have not been told the whole truth, it leads to a healthy skepticism about all of their historical education. One of Bigelow's students, named Rebecca, wrote, "What does it matter who discovered America, really? . . . But the thought that I've been lied to all my life about this, and who knows what else, really makes me angry."

This new critical thinking in schools and in colleges seems to frighten those who have glorified what is called "Western civilization." Reagan's secretary of education, William Bennett, in his 1984 "Report on the Humanities in Higher Education," writes of Western civilization as "our common culture . . . its highest ideas and aspirations." One of the most ferocious defenders of Western civilization is philosopher Allan Bloom, who wrote *The Closing of the American Mind* in the spirit of panic at what the social movements of the 1960s had done to change the educational atmosphere of American universities. He was frightened by the students demonstrations he saw at Cornell, which he saw as a terrible interference with education. Bloom's idea of education was a small group of very smart students, in an elite university, studying Plato and Aristotle and refusing to be disturbed in their contemplation by the noise outside their windows of students rallying against racism or protesting against the war in Vietnam.

As I read Bloom, I was reminded of some of my colleagues, when I was teaching in a black college in Atlanta, Georgia, at the time of the civil rights movement, who shook their heads in disapproval when our students left their classes to participate in sit-ins protesting racial segregation and be arrested. These students were neglecting their education, they said. In fact, these students were learning more in a few weeks of participation in social struggle than they could learn in a year of going to class. What a narrow, stunted understanding of education! It corresponds perfectly to the view of history that insists that Western civilization is the summit of human achievement. As Bloom wrote in his book, "only in the Western nations, i.e. those influenced by Greek philosophy, is there some willingness to doubt the identification of the good with one's own way." Well, if this willingness to doubt is the hallmark of Greek philosophy, then Bloom and his fellow idolizers of Western civilization are ignorant of that philosophy.

If Western civilization is considered the high point of human progress, the United States is the best representative of this civilization. Here is Allan Bloom again: "This is the American moment in the world history. . . . America tells one story: the unbroken, ineluctable progress of freedom and equality. From its first settlers and its political foundings on, there has been no dispute that freedom and equality are the essence of justice for us. . . . " Yes, tell black people, Native Americans, the homeless, those without health insurance, and all the victims abroad of American foreign policy that America "tells one story . . . of freedom and equality."

Western civilization is complex. It represents many things, some decent, some horrifying. We would have to pause before celebrating it uncritically when we note that David

Duke, the Louisiana Ku Klux Klan member and ex-Nazi, says that people have got him wrong. "The common strain in my thinking," he told a reporter, "is my love for Western civilization."

We who insist on looking critically at the Columbus story, and indeed at everything in our traditional histories, are often accused of insisting on political correctness to the detriment of free speech. I find this odd. It is the guardians of the old stories, the orthodox histories, who refuse to widen the spectrum of ideas and to take in new books, new approaches, new information, new views of history. They, who claim to believe in "free markets," do not believe in a free marketplace of ideas any more than they believe in a free marketplace of goods and services. In both material goods and in ideas, they want the market to be dominated by those who have always held power and wealth. They worry that if new ideas enter the marketplace people may begin to rethink the social arrangements that have given us so much suffering, so much violence, so much war these last five hundred years of "civilization."

Of course we had all that before Columbus arrived in this hemisphere, but resources were puny, people were isolated from one another, and the possibilities were narrow. In recent centuries, however, the world has become amazingly small, our possibilities for creating a decent society have been enormously magnified, and so now the excuses for hunger, ignorance, violence, and racism no longer exist.

In rethinking our history, we are not just looking at the past but at the present, and we are trying to look at it from the point of view of those who have been left out of the benefits of so-called civilizations. It is a simple but profoundly important thing we are trying to accomplish, to look at the world from other points of view. We need to do that as we come into the twenty-first century, if we want this new century to be different, if we want it to be not an American century, or a Western century, or a white century, or a male century, or any nation's or any group's century but a century for the human race.

6
GREY MATTERS INTERVIEWS
HOWARD ZINN

✎

GREY MATTERS: I'd like to start with a question about left intellectuals in general. In a news magazine in Quebec called *L'Actualité*, there's a seven-page piece about Quebec's Marxists–Leninists of the 1970s. The journalist interviewed many of them who are now between the ages of forty-five and fifty-five and who are journalists, professors, union activists, doctors, community organizers, entrepreneurs, politicians, etc. A lot of the people who were interviewed refused to have their names published for fear of being fired or recognized. Yet, these people wanted to change the world. In the past, left intellectuals have supported the Khmer Rouge and Pol Pot in Cambodia because they were communists, or the Viet Cong in Vietnam because they were fighting American imperialism or promoting the communist regimes in Albania or China. One of the people interviewed in the article goes on to say that back then, the Left in North America had models (China,

From an interview conducted by *Grey Matters* magazine December 3, 1998. Reprinted by permission of Howard Zinn.

Albania). These models don't exist anymore. What models would you be supporting today?

ZINN: Let me first say that unless you define the Left in the United States as a very narrow group, it's fair to say that most of the people on the left have not supported Marxist bureaucracies and dictatorships around the world. That stopped really in the 1950s. It stopped with the exposé of Stalin. There was a brief period of illusion about Communist China. I think there was a falling away from that too. If you define the Left more broadly, as people who believe in both socialism and democracy, I think you'll find only a small number of people on the left who supported leaders of other countries who styled themselves Marxists but who really created bureaucratic and often brutal dictatorships. So I think it's important to make a distinction between that small number who supported left dictatorships just because they call themselves Marxists. And I think the vast majority of people on the left really repudiated Stalinism and looked toward socialism and a new world order that would be democratic and international in scope. And there's no one country in the world that leftists today, defining leftists as broadly as I did, that is looked upon as a model. I think it's fair to say that people on the left in general will find pieces of a model in this country or that country or another country but will not find in any one country an ideal society. Speaking for myself, I can see that in some of the Scandinavian countries, for instance, or in New Zealand there are many socialist features that take care of old people and children and women that go far beyond how they are taken care of in a capitalist society like the United States. I mean, those are models that could be considered part of a new social system. But I think we have yet to find a place in the world that has really combined socialism and democracy in an admirable way.

GREY MATTERS: In your book *Declarations of Independence,* you cover the ground of the Left's attachment with the socialist regimes of eastern Europe and China, as well as some of its attachment with the Spanish anarchists and others. What do you feel will be the ideological models for the Left in the future?

ZINN: That, I think, is a lot easier to define than an actual sort of historical model. You mentioned Catalonia in the early months of the Spanish Civil War, a society that George Orwell described in *Homage to Catalonia,* a remarkably egalitarian society. We have historical moments like that, moments like the Paris Commune—again, just a few months in 1871 when there was remarkable grassroots democracy in Paris. But aside from that, we haven't had any sustained example of that. But when you talk about ideological models, I think we can point to ideas that came to attention in the nineteenth century with Karl Marx and Friedrich Engels, ideas that reverberated in other parts of the world with anarchists and anarcho-syndicalism with Emma Goldman, Alexander Berkman, Peter Kropotkin and American socialists like Eugene Debs, Mother Jones, and Helen Keller. There you'll find ideological models that I think people on the left today will still find attractive.

I mean, take Karl Marx as an example. I think Marx would have been horrified by what happened in the Soviet Union—by the creation of a dictatorship that was not a dictatorship of the working class but a dictatorship of a central committee or of a politburo or even of one man. Marx saw communism as assuring individual freedom. He talked about that in the *Communist Manifesto,* and he saw the solution of the problem of economic justice as the

basis for creating political justice, equality, and true democracy. And Marx praised the Paris Commune when somebody criticized his idea of the dictatorship of the proletariat,
which on its face doesn't sound very good, particularly
today when we see the practical results of dictatorships.
But a dictatorship of the proletariat is something other
than dictatorship by a minority. He said if you want to
know what I mean by that, look at the Paris Commune.
And that was hardly a dictatorship. So Marxist ideas about
creating a new society, about eliminating the corporate
control of the economy, eliminating the anarchy of the
economic system that we have under capitalism in which
the profit motive determines who gets what in the system
don't necessarily lead to the type of dictatorship that
emerged in many so-called Marxist nations. And as a result
of the profit motive, wealth gravitates toward the top and
leaves people at the bottom bereft and people in the middle nervous. And Marx's idea of a society in which at some
point everybody would have their basic needs taken care of
is not possible but desirable. And people would contribute
to society according to their ability. They would receive
from society according to their need. There would be a
short workday because technology would be used in a
humane and just way. I think Marx's ideas about a future
society, his critique of capitalism, his vision of what a good
society would be like are very pertinent today and very
usable by people on the left along with the ideas of many
others like the ideas of the anarchists and even the ideas of
social democrats.

When I was growing up I read Upton Sinclair, who was
a socialist and who presented in his book *The Jungle* an
exposé of the stockyard conditions in Chicago at the beginning of the twentieth century. It was a novel, but at the
end of the novel Sinclair had one of his characters present

a picture of what a good society would be like. It would be a society in which the fruits of the earth would be shared in a kind of rough equality, in which corporate profit would not be the driving motive of the economic system but the needs of people would determine what was done, and in which democracy would exist and people would have a voice not just in voting and choosing political leaders but a voice in how the economic system operates. So I think all those ideas (communist, socialist, anarchist) are still relevant today and are very far removed from the kind of bureaucratic dictatorships that arose in the early and middle parts of the twentieth century that called themselves Marxist.

GREY MATTERS: After your long and distinguished academic career, you've now turned to literature, *Marx in Soho*, *Emma Goldman*, and you're preparing scripts for a documentary series as well. What are your thoughts on the role of the artist in progressive politics? Edward S. Herman and Noam Chomsky have described the terrible role that some intellectuals have played in creating the order that exists today. What would the role of art and literature be in progressive politics?

ZINN: I've always been struck by the fact that the great artists and writers have in general been outspoken in their criticism of existing society and in their longing for a different kind of society. There are exceptions of course. There are people in the arts who, like the intellectuals you talked about, became supporters of the existing order and, you might say, were bought by the existing order and contributed their services to it; there have been some artists who have done that too. Of course, we've seen filmmakers under Hitler and we've seen artists in various other countries lend themselves to support the cruel regimes that they lived under. But, for the most part, when I think of artists, I think of Tolstoy, who at a certain point in his life decided that even the great novels he had written were insufficient for helping to change the world. And so he began to write about the necessity for civil disobedience, the necessity for soldiers to disobey orders to go to war and about the needs of peasants and to plunge himself into attempts to ease the plight of peasants in Russia. I think of the artists who gave their support to the Paris Commune, of Corbet, who became one of the leaders of the Paris Commune.

In modern times, I think of Sartre and Camus, who, although they disagreed on various things, both lent their names and their art to antifascism and to the idea of creating a good society. I've always been impressed by dramatists with social vision: Chekov and Gogol, and in this country, people like Arthur Miller and Lillian Hellman, and musicians, singers, and poets. And I think of the black struggle in this country and the role that people played: Paul Robeson, Langston Hughes. They were not content with writing poetry or singing songs that would simply please and entertain people. They wanted their poems and their songs to play some part in the social struggle of our time.

So in general, I see artists as playing a positive role and a very special role because art has the capacity of taking ideas that otherwise would be kind of dry and unappealing and infusing those ideas with a kind of passion that music, poetry, fiction, the theatre, and painting can convey. Art, therefore, because it has that power, the special power of enhancing the strength of an idea with emotion, is an attempt to equalize a situation in which most of the material power, the military power, the economic power rests in the hands of the establishment. Therefore the people without power—the people on the outside, the people without the money, the people without the guns, the people who are trying to form a social movement—have a great need of art to mobilize people, to inspire people and to do what mere words on paper, mere pamphlets and books, cannot do by themselves.

GREY MATTERS: Art allows the emotional revolution and emotional resistance to the structures of power.

ZINN: When you read the autobiography of Emma Goldman, it's not simply a recounting of her life. My experience has been that I would give her autobiography to my students to read and it was obvious that they were not just reading a narrative of her life, a recounting of her experiences. They were being uplifted, they were being inspired by what this woman went through, by what she stood for, by her courage, by her defiance of existing authority. It was an emotional experience to read her autobiography.

GREY MATTERS: You talked about Emma Goldman and her resisting of authority. In your book *Declarations of Independence,* you say that "absolute obedience to law may bring order temporarily but it may not bring justice." I was wondering when and why we should not obey the law and where we should focus our disobedience toward the law today.

ZINN: The principle of civil disobedience doesn't state as a universal that you must always disobey the law. What it does do is refuse the universal principle that you must always obey the law. And what it does is declare a willingness to decide when laws are consonant with morality and when laws are immoral and support terrible things like war, racism, or sexism. And so laws that sustain injustice should be disobeyed. Sometimes, though, it's the law itself that's disobeyed, sometimes the law that is disobeyed is a law against trespassing or a law against picketing and people will commit civil disobedience and trespass, as the sit-down strikers did in the United States in the 1930s when they took over factories or as the black protesters did in the civil rights movement in the United States when they sat down at lunch counters and refused to move. But the idea of civil disobedience is that Law is not sacrosanct. Law, after all, is not made by God, it's not made by any holy authority. Law is made by men, mostly men, very few women involved, men who are in power and who don't dispense the law as an objective representation of democratic ideas but who pass laws according to their own interests.

The best proof of this is to simply look at the laws that are actually passed by legislatures in modern societies. If you look at the laws passed in the United States from the very beginning of the American republic down to the present day, you'll find that most of the legislation passed is class legislation that favors the elite, that favors the rich. You'll find huge subsidies to corporations all through American history. You'll find legislation passed to benefit the railroads, the oil companies, and the merchant marine and very little legislation passed to benefit the poor and the people who desperately need help. So the Law should not be given the holy deference that we are all taught to give it when we grow up and go to school, and it's a profoundly undemocratic idea to say that you should judge what you do according to what the Law says—undemocratic because it divests you as an individual of the right to make a decision yourself about what is right or wrong and it gives all of that power to that small band of legislators who have decided for themselves what is right and what is wrong.

So to me the idea of civil disobedience is to really enhance democracy, to give people out of power a weapon with which to batter against the pillars of the society. And the best way to understand civil disobedience is simply to look at it historically, to look at the way it was used by working people in the fight for the eight-hour day, the way it's used in strike situations, the way it's used by black people in the struggle against racial segregation, the way it was used by people who were fighting against the Vietnam War or women who are struggling for equality. And today, right now in the United States, there are acts of civil disobedience going on at all levels. Just a few examples: people have been going into nuclear plants where nuclear weapons are being manufactured and committing acts of civil disobedience, engaging in little token acts of sabotage to try to draw attention to the enormous military budget of the United States and the militarization of the country. Recently, at Fort Benning, Georgia, where the School of the Americas trains Latin American police officers and army personnel and has a terrible record of training torturers and members of death squads, people have been protesting and getting arrested throughout the 1980s and also in the 1990s. Just last week [November 1998] several thousand people were demonstrating at Fort Benning against the School of the Americas. Phil Berrigan is one of the number of people protesting who committed civil disobedience against a nuclear armed destroyer in Bath, Maine. And he and others were arrested, but they wanted to bring the attention of the country to the fact that we are still, despite the nonexistence of the Soviet Union, engaging in a kind of bizarre expenditure of the wealth of the United States to build a monstrous military machine. At the end of November 1998, people in Boston committed acts of civil disobedience by going into the State House and refusing to leave because they were protesting the fact that welfare benefits for thousands of poor people in Massachusetts were going to be cut off as a result of the so-called welfare-reform act that was passed by both Clinton and the Republicans in 1995. So civil disobedience is very much alive as a way of protesting injustice.

GREY MATTERS: I have to say that I was particularly impressed by your description in your book *Declarations of Independence* of the way civil disobedience has been the key tool to provoke change within the American political system for the last several hundred years. The popular myths of certain freedoms were in no way comparable in their effectiveness when compared to the acts, and sometimes the very dangerous acts, of civil disobedience that courageous people stood for.

ZINN: I think that the history of the United States indicates that the redressing of serious grievances has not been done by the three branches of government that are always paraded before junior high school students and high school students as the essence of democracy. It hasn't been Congress or the president or the Supreme Court who has initiated acts to remedy racial inequality or economic injustice, or to do something about the government going to war. It's always taken the actions of citizens and actions of civil disobedience to bring these issues to national attention and finally force the president, Congress, and the Supreme Court to begin to move. You were talking about this going on for hundreds of years. If you go back one hundred and fifty years ago to the middle of the nineteenth century, to the 1850s, you'll see that it wasn't Lincoln who caused the antislavery sentiment in the country to grow. Lincoln was reacting to the growth of the movement that became stronger and stronger from the 1830s to the outbreak of the Civil War and in the 1850s manifested itself in many acts of civil disobedience against the

Fugitive Slave Act that had been passed in 1850. The Fugitive Slave Act required the federal government to aid southern slave owners in bringing escaped slaves back to the South. Well, people in the North—escaped slaves, free black people, white people—gathered together in committees. They broke into courthouses and into jailhouses to rescue escaped slaves. And they certainly used acts of civil disobedience. And in a number of cases when they were brought up on charges and put on trial, juries acquitted them, because juries recognized the morality of what these protesters were doing even though they had broken the law.

GREY MATTERS: The Left used to speak about the insoluble crisis of capitalism and trying to oppose it in some way. Yet despite the fall of communism, capitalism is still here. I was wondering what kind of spiritual reawakening or changes in our way of thinking should occur in order to make issues such as the inequalities of the current system appear in the mainstream media?

ZINN: There's an enormous job of education that needs to be done, and this will have to be done in spite of the control of the media by these new media giants that control the press, the television stations, the radio stations, and the major newspapers of the country. And yet, we've had this experience before. That is where social movements have brought their demands to the attention of the nation, even though they did not control the press and the means of communication. And they did it by organizing around the country, by raising their voices, through dramatic events, by committing acts of civil disobedience, through demonstrations, protests, boycotts, and strikes, and by educating the public in words and in action. And I think that the public in the United States is ready to listen to ideas about a new way of ordering society. I say ready because I think there's a general dissatisfaction with the American political system. There's an understanding among Americans that the political system doesn't work. That's why 50 percent of the electorate does not go to the polls. And of those that do go to the polls, there's a distinct lack of enthusiasm. There's an understanding that the domination of the political process by the two major parties in the United States doesn't allow for different kinds of opinions, different kinds of voices, different kinds of political alternatives. If you look at public opinion surveys in the United States over the past five or ten years, you'll find an interesting thing, and that is that public opinion surveys show that the American people as a whole are far more progressive than either of the major parties. You'll find again and again that the American public wants the government to intervene in the economy on behalf of people who are in need. You'll find that they want the government to tax the rich more heavily, that they're opposed to reducing the taxes on capital gains, which benefits the wealthiest portion of the country. Again and again, the public has said in these polls that they would like to see a new independent political force other than the Democrats and the Republicans enter the contest for political office. So, on the one hand, the system goes along concentrating more and more wealth at the top and more and more power at the top, and then, on the other hand, there's this reservoir of opposition in the country that has not yet organized itself into a political force. And I think that it will take a lot more education and a lot more connections made among the millions of people in this country who want to change before something important and dramatic happens.

GREY MATTERS: As a concluding question, can you give us a few words on your own personal dedication to these causes over the last forty or more years? You've worked in the South in the great desegregation struggles, during the Vietnam War, throughout the 1970s. How do you continue your work with the same dedication toward progressive change without falling into cynicism or despair?

ZINN: Well, I think what sustains me is that I'm in contact with a lot of people around the country. I go around the country and do a lot of speaking, I go to all sorts of places all over the United States, and wherever I go, I see people who are trying to do something about justice. Wherever I go, I see people struggling: women struggling for equal rights, people working against racial discrimination, gay and lesbian people organizing for their rights, people protesting against foreign policy. Wherever I go, I see this. And wherever I go, I meet wonderful people, and however small the town is that I'm going into, there's always a cluster of really good people who've devoted themselves to social change. Now this encourages me; this keeps me going. And this is in the immediate sense. But I think what also keeps me going is a kind of sense of history. There's a recognition that, although cynicism and pessimism are sort of natural feelings when you look around at any given moment and see that things don't seem to be changing, those feelings of cynicism and pessimism have existed all through American history, in every period. And yet, at certain moments in history when people begin to speak up, when people begin to get together at certain moments of history, suddenly there's a breakthrough and something happens. It happened in the 1930s with the rise of the labor movement, and it happened in the 1960s with the civil rights, antiwar, and women's movements. And I think a little historical perspective would dispel some of the pessimism. People would realize that in the years before the rise of any of these movements, everything looked gloomy and then, suddenly, things began to happen. Things can happen very fast when the indignation of the people overflows and when they begin to get together.

I'll say just one more thing, and that is: One of the things that makes me continue to speak out and to try to be active and involved is simply that it makes life more interesting and more enjoyable, it makes life more worthwhile. I think of Tolstoy and his story of the death of Ivan Ilyich, about this very successful man on his deathbed who asks the questions, "Have I done all the right things? I've become prosperous and successful and respected by society. Why am I dissatisfied?" He was dissatisfied because he hadn't really done anything important to change the world. And I think people who are involved lead more fruitful and more fulfilling lives. So that's what sustains me.

7
BEING LEFT:
GROWING UP CLASS-CONSCIOUS

⟜

I was in my teens when I wrote this poem:

> Go see your Uncle Phil
> And say hello.
> Who would walk a mile today
> To say hello,
> The city freezing in the snow
> Phil had a news stand
> Under the black El.
> He sat on a wooden box
> In the cold and in the heat.
> And three small rooms across the street.
> Today the wooden box was gone,
> On top the stand Uncle Phil was curled,
> A skeleton inside an Army coat.
> He smiled and gave me a stick of gum

This chapter appeared in an earlier form as part of chapter 13 in *You Can't Be Neutral on a Moving Train: A Personal History of Our Times* by Howard Zinn (Boston: Beacon Press, 1994). Copyright © 1994 by Howard Zinn. Reprinted by permission of the author and Beacon Press, Boston.

With stiffened fingers, red and numb.
Go see your Uncle Phil today
My mother said again in June
I walked the mile to say hello
With the city smelling almost sweet
Brand new sneakers on my feet.
The stand was nailed and boarded tight
And quiet in the sun.
Uncle Phil lay cold, asleep,
Under the black El, in a wooden box
In three small rooms across the street.

I recall this certainly not as an example of "poetry" but because it evokes something about my growing up in the slums of Brooklyn in the 1930s, when my father and mother, in desperate moments, turned to saviors: the corner grocer, who gave credit by writing down the day's purchases on a roll of paper; the kind doctor who treated my rickets for years without charging; Uncle Phil, whose army service earned him a newsstand license, who loaned us money when we had trouble paying the rent.

Phil and my father were two of four brothers, Jewish immigrants from Austria, who came to this country before the First World War and worked together in New York factories. My father, looking to escape the factory, became a waiter who worked mostly at weddings and sometimes in restaurants and a member of Local 2 of the Waiters Union. While the union tightly controlled its membership, on New Year's Eve, when there was a need for extra waiters, the sons of the members, called "Juniors," would work alongside their fathers, and I did too.

I hated every moment of it. The ill-fitting waiter's tuxedo, borrowed from my father, the sleeves absurdly short (my father was five-foot-five and at sixteen I was a six-footer). The way the bosses treated the waiters, who were fed chicken wings just before they marched out to serve roast beef and filet mignon to the guests. Everybody in their fancy dress, wearing silly hats, singing "Auld Lang Syne" as the New Year began, and me standing there in my waiter's costume, watching my father, his face strained, clear his tables, feeling no joy at the coming of the New Year.

My father's name was Eddie. In the Depression years, the weddings fell off, there was little work, and he got tired of hanging around the union hall playing cards waiting for a job. So he became, at different times, a window cleaner, a pushcart peddler, a street necktie salesman, and a WPA worker in Central Park. As a window cleaner, his supporting belt broke one day, and he fell off the ladder onto the concrete steps of a subway entrance. I was perhaps twelve, and I remember him being brought, bleeding, into our little flat. He had hurt himself badly. My mother would not let him clean windows again.

All his life my father worked hard for very little. I've always resented the smug statements of politicians, media commentators, and corporate executives who talked of how, in America, if you worked hard, you would become rich. I knew this was a lie, about my father and millions of others, men and women, who worked harder than anyone, harder than financiers and politicians, harder than anybody if you accepted that when you worked at an unpleasant job that made it very hard work indeed.

My mother worked and worked, without getting paid at all. She had grown up in Irkutsk, in Siberia. While my father worked his hours on the job, she worked all day and all night, managing the family, finding the food, cooking and cleaning, and taking the kids to the doctor or the hospital clinic for measles and mumps and whooping cough and tonsillitis and whatever came up. She also took care of family finances. My father had a fourth-grade education and could not read much or do much arithmetic. My mother had gone as far as the seventh grade, but her intelligence went far beyond that; she was the brains and strength of the family.

Her name was Jenny. She told of her mother's arranged marriage in Irkutsk: "They brought a boy home, a Jewish soldier stationed in Irkutsk, and said, this is who you'll marry." They immigrated to America. Her mother died in her thirties, having given birth to three boys and three girls, and her father—against whom she boiled with indignation all her life—deserted the family. Jenny, the eldest but only a teenager, became the mother of the family, taking care of her siblings by working in factories until they grew up and found jobs.

Jenny met Eddie through his sister, who worked in her factory, and it was a passionate marriage all the way. Eddie died at sixty-seven. To the end he was carrying trays of food at weddings and restaurants, never having made enough money to retire. My mother outlived him by many years. She lived by herself, fiercely insisting on her independence, knitting sweaters for everybody, saving shopping coupons, playing bingo with her friends. But toward the end she suffered a stroke and entered a nursing home.

We lived in a succession of tenements, sometimes four rooms, sometimes three. Some winters we lived in a building with central heating. Other times, we lived in what was called "a cold-water flat"—no heat except from the coal cooking stove in the kitchen, no hot water except what we boiled on that same stove.

It was always a battle to pay the bills. I would come home from school in the winter, when the sun set at four, and find the house dark—the electric company had turned off the electricity, and my mother would be sitting, knitting by candlelight.

There was no refrigerator but an icebox, for which we would go to the "ice dock" and buy a five-cent or ten-cent chunk of ice. In the winter a wooden box rested on the sill just outside the window, using nature to keep things cold. There was no shower, but the washtub in the kitchen was our bathtub.

No radio for a long time, until one day my father took me on a long walk through the city to find a second-hand radio and triumphantly brought it home on his shoulder, with me trotting along by his side. No telephone. We would be called to the phone at the candy store down the block and pay the kid who ran upstairs to get us two pennies or a nickel. Sometimes we hung out near the phone to take the call and race to collect the nickel.

I don't remember ever being hungry. The rent might not be paid (we moved often, a step ahead of eviction). No bills might be paid. But my mother was ingenious at making sure there was always food: always hot cereal in the morning, always hot soup in the evening, always bread, butter, eggs, milk, noodles, cheese, sour cream, chicken fricassee.

My mother was not shy about using the English language, which she adapted to her purposes. We would hear her telling her friend about the problem she was having with "very close veins," or "a pain in my crutch." She would look in the dairy store for "monster cheese." She would say to my father, if he forgot something, "Eddie, try to remember, wreck your brains."

We four boys grew up together sleeping two or three to a bed, in rooms dark and uninviting. So I spent a lot of time in the street or the schoolyard, playing handball, football, softball, and stickball or taking boxing lessons from the guy in the neighborhood who had made the Golden Gloves and was our version of a celebrity.

In the time I did spend in the house, I read. From the time I was eight I read whatever books I could find. The very first I picked up on the street. The beginning pages were torn out, but that didn't matter. It was *Tarzan and the Jewels of Opar,* and from then on I was a fan of Edgar Rice Burroughs, a fan of not only his Tarzan books but also his other fantasies: *The Chessmen of Mars,* about the way wars were fought by Martians, with warriors on foot or on horses playing out the chess moves; *At the Earth's Core,* about a strange civilization in the center of the earth.

There were no books in our house. My father had never read a book. My mother read romance magazines. They both read the newspaper. They knew little about politics, except that Franklin Roosevelt was a good man because he helped the poor.

As a boy I read no children's books. My parents did not know about such books. But when I was ten, the *New York Post* offered a set of the complete works of Charles Dickens (of whom they had never heard, of course). By using coupons cut out of the newspaper, they could get a volume every week for a few pennies. So they signed up, because they knew I loved to read. And so I read Dickens in the order in which we received the books, starting with *David Copperfield* and working my way through *Oliver Twist, Great Expectations, The Pickwick Papers, Hard Times, A Tale of Two Cities,* and all the rest, until the coupons were exhausted and so was I.

I did not know where Dickens fit into the history of modern literature because he was all I knew of that literature. What I did know was that he aroused in me tumultuous emotions. First, an anger at arbitrary power puffed up with wealth and kept in place by law. But most of all a profound compassion for the poor. I did not see myself as poor in the way Oliver Twist was poor. I didn't recognize that I was so moved by his story because his life touched chords in mine.

For my thirteenth birthday my parents, knowing that I was writing things in notebooks, bought me a rebuilt Underwood typewriter. It came with a practice book for learning the touch system, and soon I was typing book reviews for everything I read and keeping them in my drawer. I never showed them to anyone. It gave me joy and pride just to know that I had read these books and could write about them on a typewriter.

From the age of fourteen I had after-school and summer jobs—delivering clothes for a dry cleaner, working as a caddy on a golf course in Queens. I also helped out in a succession of candy stores my parents bought in a desperate attempt to make enough money so my father could quit being a waiter. The stores all failed, but my three younger brothers and I had lots of milk shakes, ice cream, and candy while the shops existed.

I remember the last of those candy-store situations, and it was typical. The six of us lived above the store in a four-room flat in a dirty, old five-story tenement on Bushwick Avenue in Brooklyn. The street was always full of life, especially in spring and summer, when everyone seemed to be outside: old folks sitting on chairs, mothers holding their babies, teenagers playing ball, the "older guys" throwing the bull, fooling with girls.

I especially remember that time because I was seventeen and had begun to be interested in world politics. I was reading books about fascism in Europe. George Seldes's *Sawdust Caesar,* about Mussolini's seizure of power in Italy, fascinated me. I could not get out of my mind the courage of Socialist Deputy Giacomo Matteotti, who defied

Mussolini and was dragged from his home and killed by brown-shirted thugs.

I read something called *The Brown Book of the Nazi Terror*, which described what was happening in Germany under Hitler. It was a drama beyond anything a playwright or novelist could imagine. And now the Nazi war machine was beginning to move: into the Rhineland, Austria, Czechoslovakia. The newspapers and radio were full of excitement: Chamberlain meeting Hitler at Munich, the sudden, astonishing nonaggression pact of the two archenemies, Soviet Russia and Nazi Germany. And, finally, the invasion of Poland and the start of World War II.

The Civil War in Spain, just ended with victory for the fascist general Franco, seemed the event closest to all of us, because several thousand American radicals—communists, socialists, anarchists—had crossed the Atlantic to fight with the democratic government of Spain. A young fellow who played street football with us—short and thin, the fastest runner in the neighborhood—disappeared. Months later, the word came to us: Jerry had gone to Spain to fight against Franco.

On Bushwick Avenue, among the basketball players and street talkers, there were some young communists a few years older than me. They had jobs, but after work and on weekends they distributed Marxist literature in the neighborhood and talked politics into the night with whoever was interested.

I was interested. I was reading about what was happening in the world. I argued with the communist guys, especially about the Russian invasion of Finland. They insisted it was necessary for the Soviet Union to protect itself against future attack, but to me it was a brutal act of aggression against a tiny country, and none of their carefully worked out justifications persuaded me.

Still, I agreed with them on lots of things. They were ferociously antifascist, indignant as I was about the contrasts of wealth and poverty in America. I admired them—they seemed to know so much about politics, economics, what was happening everywhere in the world. And they were courageous—I had seen them defy the local police, who tried to stop them from distributing literature on the street or to break up their knots of discussion. Besides, they were regular guys, good athletes.

One summer day they asked me if I wanted to go with them to "a demonstration" that evening. I had never been to such a thing. I made some excuse to my parents, and a bunch of us took the subway to Times Square. When we arrived, it was just a typical evening in Times Square—the streets crowded, the lights glittering. "Where's the demonstration?" I asked my friend Leon. He was tall, blond, the ideal "Aryan" type, but the son of German communists who were also nature-worshippers and part of a little colony of health-conscious German socialists out in the New Jersey countryside.

"Wait," he said. "Ten o'clock." We continued to stroll among the crowd.

As the clock on the tower struck ten, the scene changed. In the midst of the crowd, banners were unfurled and people, perhaps a thousand or more, formed into lines carrying banners and signs and chanting slogans about peace and justice and a dozen other causes of the day. It was exciting. And nonthreatening. All these people were keeping to the sidewalks, not blocking traffic, walking in orderly, nonviolent lines through Times Square. My friend and I were walking behind two women carrying a banner, and he said: "Let's relieve them." So we each took an end of the banner. I felt a bit like Charlie Chaplin in *Modern Times* when he casually picked up a red signal flag and suddenly found a thousand people marching behind him with raised fists.

We heard sirens, and I thought: there must be a fire somewhere, an accident of some kind. But then I heard screams and saw hundreds of police, mounted on horses and on foot, charging into the lines of marchers, smashing people with their clubs. I was astonished, bewildered. This was America, a country where, whatever its faults, people could speak, write, assemble, and demonstrate without fear. It was in the Constitution, the Bill of Rights. We were a democracy.

As I absorbed this, as my thoughts raced, all in a few seconds, I was spun around by a very large man who seized my shoulder and hit me very hard. I only saw him as a blur. I didn't know whether he hit me with a club or a fist or a blackjack, but I was knocked unconscious.

I awoke in a doorway perhaps a half hour later. I had no sense of how much time had elapsed, but it was an eerie scene I woke up to. There was no demonstration going on, there were no police in sight, my friend Leon was gone, and Times Square was filled with its usual Saturday night crowd—as if nothing had happened, as if it was all a dream. But I knew it wasn't a dream. There was a painful lump on the side of my head.

More important, there was a very painful thought in my head: those young communists on the block were right. The state and its police were not neutral referees in a society of contending interests. They were on the side of the rich and powerful. Free speech? Try it, and the police will be there with their horses, their clubs, and their guns to stop you.

From that moment on, I was no longer a liberal, a believer in the self-correcting character of American democracy. I was a radical, believing that something fundamental was wrong in this country—not just the existence of poverty amid great wealth, not just the horrible treatment of black people, but something rotten at the root. The situation required not just a new president or new laws but an uprooting of the old order, the introduction of a new kind of society—cooperative, peaceful, egalitarian.

Perhaps I am exaggerating the importance of that one experience. But I think not. I have come to believe that our lives can be turned in a different direction by, our minds adopt a different way of thinking through, some significant, though small, event. That belief can be frightening, or exhilarating, depending on whether you just contemplate it or do something with it.

The years following that experience in Times Square might be called "my communist years." That would be easy to misunderstand, because the word "communist" conjures up Joseph Stalin and the gulags of death and torture, the disappearance of free expression, the atmosphere of fear and trembling created in the Soviet Union, the ugly bureaucracy that lasted seventy years pretending to be "socialism."

None of that was in the minds or intentions of the young working-class people I knew who called themselves "communists." Certainly not in my mind. Little was known about the Soviet Union except the romantic image, popularized by people like the English theologian the Dean of Canterbury. In his book *The Soviet Power,* distributed widely by the communist movement, he gave idealists disillusioned with capitalism the vision they longed for: of a place where the country belonged to "the people," where everyone had work and free health care, women had equal opportunities with men, and a hundred different ethnic groups were treated with respect.

The Soviet Union was this romantic blur, far away. What was close at hand, visible, was that communists were the leaders in organizing working people all over the country. They were the most daring, risking arrest and beatings to organize auto workers in Detroit, steel workers in Pittsburgh, textile workers in North Carolina, fur and leather workers in New York, and longshoremen on the West Coast. They were the first to speak up, more than that, to demonstrate, to chain themselves to factory gates and White House fences, when blacks were lynched in the South, when the "Scottsboro Boys" were being railroaded to prison in Alabama.

My image of "a communist" was not a Soviet bureaucrat but my friend Leon's father, a cabdriver who came home from work bruised and bloody one day, beaten up by his employer's goons (yes, that word was soon part of my vocabulary) for trying to organize his fellow cabdrivers into a union.

Everyone knew that the communists were the first antifascists, protesting against Mussolini's invasion of Ethiopia and Hitler's persecution of the Jews. And, most impressive of all, it was the communists, thousands of them, who volunteered to fight in Spain, in the Abraham Lincoln Brigade, to join volunteers from all over the world to defend Madrid and the Spanish people against the fascist army of Francisco Franco, which was given arms and airplanes by Germany and Italy.

Furthermore, some of the best people in the country were connected with the communist movement in some way; there were heroes and heroines one could admire. There was Paul Robeson, the fabulous singer-actor-athlete, whose magnificent voice could fill Madison Square Garden, crying out against racial injustice, against fascism. And literary figures (weren't Theodore Dreiser and W. E. B. Du Bois communists?), and talented, socially conscious Hollywood actors and writers and directors (yes, "The Hollywood Ten," hauled before a Congressional Committee, defended by Humphrey Bogart and so many others).

True, in that movement, as in any other, you could see the righteousness leading to dogmatism, the closed circle of ideas impermeable by doubt, an intolerance of dissent by people who were the most persecuted of dissenters. But however imperfect, even repugnant sometimes, particular policies or particular actions were, there remained the purity of the ideal, represented in the theories of Karl Marx and the noble visions of many lesser thinkers and writers.

I remember my first reading of the *Communist Manifesto*, which Marx and Engels wrote when they too were young radicals; Marx was thirty, Engels, twenty-eight. "The history of all hitherto existing society is the history of class struggle." That was undeniably true, verifiable in any reading of history. Certainly true for the United States, despite all the pretensions of the Constitution ("We, the People of the United States . . ." and "No state shall . . . deny to any person . . . the equal protection of the laws.").

Marx and Engels's analysis of capitalism made sense, its history of exploitation, its creation of extremes of wealth and poverty, even in the liberal "democracy" of this country. And their socialist vision was not one of dictatorship or bureaucracy but of a free society. Their "dictatorship of the proletariat" was a transitional phase, in which society would go from a dictatorship of the rich to a dictatorship of the poor to a classless society of true democracy, true freedom.

A rational, just economic system would allow a short workday and leave everyone free to do as they liked—to write poetry, to be in nature, to play sports, to be truly human, to fulfill their potentiality as human beings. Nationalism would be a thing of the past. People all over the world, of whatever race, of whatever continent, would live in peace and cooperation.

In my teenage reading, those ideas were kept alive by some of the finest writers in America. I read Upton Sinclair's

The Jungle. Work in the Chicago stockyards was the epitome of capitalist exploitation. And in the last pages of the book, the vision of a new society is thrilling. John Steinbeck's *The Grapes of Wrath* was an eloquent cry against the conditions of life where the poor were expendable and any attempt on their part to change their lives was met with police clubs.

When I was eighteen, unemployed, my family desperate for help, I took a much-publicized civil service examination for a job in the Brooklyn Navy Yard. Thirty thousand young men (women applicants were unthinkable) took the exam, competing for a few hundred jobs. It was 1940, and New Deal programs had relieved but not ended the Depression. When the results were announced, four hundred of the applicants had gotten a score of 100 percent on the exam and would get jobs. I was one of them. For me and my family, it was a triumph. My salary would be $14.40 for a forty-hour week. I could give the family ten dollars a week and have the rest for lunch and spending money.

It was also an introduction to the world of heavy industry. I was to be an apprentice shipfitter for the next three years. I would work out "on the ways," a vast inclined surface at the edge of the harbor on which a battleship, the USS *Iowa*, was to be built. (Many years later, in the 1980s, I was called to be a witness at a trial in Staten Island of pacifists who had demonstrated against the placement of nuclear weapons on a battleship docked there—the USS *Iowa*.) Our job, basically, was to fit together the steel plates of the hull, doing a lot of crawling around inside the tiny steel compartments of the "inner bottom," where smells and sounds were magnified a hundred times. We measured and hammered, and cut and welded, using the service of "burners" and "chippers."

There were no women workers. The skilled jobs were held by white men, who were organized in AFL craft unions known to be inhospitable to blacks. The few blacks in the shipyard had the toughest, most physically demanding, jobs, like the riveters.

What made the job bearable was the steady pay and the accompanying dignity of being a working man, bringing home money like my father. There was also the pride that we were doing something for the war effort. But most important was that I found a small group of friends, fellow apprentices—some of them shipfitters like myself, others shipwrights, machinists, pipefitters, sheet metal workers, and so on—who were young radicals, determined to do something to change the world. No less.

We were excluded from the craft unions of the skilled workers, so we decided to organize the apprentices into a union, an association. We would act together to improve our working conditions, raise our pay, and create a camaraderie during and after working hours to add some fun to our workaday lives.

This we did, successfully, with three hundred young workers, and for me it was an introduction to actual participation in a labor movement. We were organizing a union and doing what working people had done through the centuries, creating little spaces of culture and friendship to make up for the dreariness of the work itself.

Four of us, who were elected as officers of the Apprentice Association, became special friends. We met one evening a week to read books on politics and economics and talk about world affairs. These were years when some fellows our age were in college, but we felt we were getting a good education.

Still, I was glad to leave the shipyard and join the air force. It was while flying combat missions in Europe that I began to have a sharp turn in my political thinking, away from the romanticization of the Soviet Union that enveloped many radicals and others too—especially in the atmosphere of World War II and the stunning successes of the Red Army against the Nazi invaders. The reason for this turn was my encounter with an aerial gunner on another crew who questioned whether the aims of the allies—England, France, the United States, the Soviet Union—were really antifascist and democratic.

One book he gave me shook forever ideas I had held for years. This was *The Yogi and the Commissar* by Arthur Koestler. Koestler had been a communist, had fought in Spain, but had become convinced—and his factual evidence was powerful, his logic unshakable—that the Soviet Union, with its claims to be a "socialist" state, was a fraud. (After the war, I read *The God That Failed,* in which writers whose integrity and dedication to justice I could not question—Richard Wright, André Gide, Ignazio Silone, and Koestler too—described their loss of faith in the communist movement and the Soviet Union.)

Disillusionment with the Soviet Union did not diminish my belief in socialism any more than disillusionment with the U.S. government lessened my belief in democracy. It certainly did not affect my consciousness of class, of the difference in the way rich and poor lived in the United States, in the failure of the society to provide the most basic biological necessities—food, housing, health care—to tens of millions of people.

Oddly enough, when I became a second lieutenant in the army air corps, I got a taste of what life was like for the privileged classes—for now I had better clothes, better food, more money, higher status than I had had in civilian life.

After the war, with a few hundred dollars in mustering-out money and my uniform and medals packed away, I rejoined my wife, Roslyn. We were a young, happy married couple. But we could find no other place to live but a rat-infested basement apartment in Bedford-Stuyvesant.

I was back in the working class, but needing a job. I tried going back to the Brooklyn Navy Yard, but it was hateful work with none of the compensating features of that earlier time. I worked as a waiter, as a ditchdigger, and as a brewery worker, and I collected unemployment insurance in between jobs. (I can understand very well the feelings of veterans of the Vietnam War, who were important when soldiers but came back home with no jobs, no prospects, and without the glow that surrounded the veterans of World War II—a diminishing of their selves.) In the meantime, our daughter Myla was born.

At the age of twenty-seven, with a second child on the way, I began college as a freshman at New York University under the GI Bill of Rights. That gave me four years of free college education and $120 a month, so that with Roz working part time, with Myla and Jeff in nursery, and with me working a night shift after school, we could survive.

Whenever I hear that the government must not get involved in helping people, that this must be left to "private enterprise," I think of the GI Bill and its marvelous nonbureaucratic efficiency. There are certain necessities—housing, medical care, education—about which private enterprise doesn't give a hoot (because supplying these to the poor is not profitable, and private enterprise won't act without profit).

Starting college coincided with a change in our lives: moving out of our miserable basement rooms into a low-income housing project in downtown Manhattan on the East River. Four rooms, utilities included in the rent, no rats, no cockroaches, a few trees and a playground downstairs, a park along the river. We were happy.

While going to NYU and Columbia, I worked the four-to-twelve shift in the basement of a Manhattan warehouse, loading heavy cartons of clothing onto trailer trucks that would carry them to cities all over the country. We were an odd crew, we warehouse loaders—a black man, a Honduran immigrant, another veteran of the war (married, with children, he sold his blood to supplement his small pay check). With us for a while was a young man named Jeff Lawson, whose father was John Howard Lawson, a Hollywood writer, one of the Hollywood Ten. There was another young man, a Columbia College student, who was named after his grandfather, the socialist labor leader Daniel De Leon (I encountered him many years later; he was in a bad way mentally, and then I got word that he had laid down under his car in the garage and breathed in enough carbon monoxide to kill himself).

We were all members of the union, District 65, which had a reputation of being a "left-wing" union. But we, the truck-loaders, were more left than the union, which seemed hesitant to interfere with the loading operation of this warehouse. We were angry about our working conditions, having to load outside on the sidewalk in rain or snow, with no rain or snow gear available to us. We kept asking the company for gear, with no results. One night, late, the rain began pelting down. We stopped work, said we would not continue unless we had a binding promise of rain gear. The supervisor was beside himself. The truck had to get out that night to meet the schedule, he told us. He had no authority to promise anything. We said, tough shit. We're not getting drenched for the damned schedule. He got on the phone, nervously called a company executive at his home, interrupting a dinner party. He came back from the phone. "Okay, you'll get your gear." The next workday, we arrived at the warehouse and found a line of shiny new raincoats and rainhats.

That was my world for the first thirty-three years of my life—the world of unemployment and bad employment, of me and Roz leaving our two- and three-year-olds in the care of others while we went to school or to work, living most of that time in cramped and unpleasant places, hesitating to call the doctor when the children were sick because we couldn't afford to pay him, finally taking the children to hospital clinics where interns could take care of them. That is the way a large part of the population lives, even in this, the richest country in the world. And when, armed with the proper degrees, I began to move out of that world, becoming a college professor, I never forgot that. I never stopped being class-conscious.

I note how our political leaders step gingerly around such expressions, how it seems the worst accusation one politician can make about another is that "he appeals to class hostility, he is setting class against class." Well, class has been set against class, not in words but in the realities of life, for a very long time, and the words will disappear only when the realities of inequity disappear.

It would be foolish for me to claim that class consciousness was simply the result of growing up poor and living the life of a poor kid and then the life of a hard-pressed young husband and father. There are many people with similar backgrounds who developed a very different set of ideas about society. And there are many others, whose early lives were much different than mine, whose worldview was close to mine.

When I was chair of the history department at Spelman College and I had the power (even a little power can make people heady) to hire one or two people, I invited Staughton Lynd, a brilliant young historian, graduate of Harvard and Columbia, to join the Spelman faculty. We were introduced at a historians' meeting in New York, where Staughton expressed a desire to teach at a black college.

Staughton came from a background completely different from mine. His parents were quite famous professors at Columbia and Sarah Lawrence, Robert and Helen Lynd, authors of the sociological classic *Middletown*. Staughton had been raised in comfortable circumstances, had gone to Harvard and Columbia. And yet, as we went back and forth on every political issue under the sun—race, class, war, violence, nationalism, justice, fascism, capitalism, socialism, and more—it was clear that our social philosophies, our values, were extraordinarily similar.

In the light of such experiences, traditional dogmatic "class analysis" cannot remain intact. But as dogma disintegrates, hope appears. Because it seems that human beings, whatever their backgrounds, are more open than we think, that their behavior cannot be confidently predicted from their past, that we are all creatures vulnerable to new thoughts, new attitudes. While such vulnerability creates all sorts of possibilities, both good and bad, its very existence is exciting. It means that no human being should be written off, no change in thinking should be deemed impossible.

8
WHAT BUSH'S WAR ON TERROR IS
ALL ABOUT

ᳵ

ARNOVE: George W. Bush is beating the drums of war to invade Iraq. Why is this happening now? Is the war that they're planning on Iraq about oil?

ZINN: Why now? I think it's because the "war on terrorism" looks more and more to the American public—and certainly to the world—as, at best, unsuccessful, and, at worst, a sham.

The bombing of Afghanistan has gone on for almost a year, and we see no sign of Osama bin Laden and no indications that we've uprooted any terrorist networks. So the Bush administration needs to turn the attention from a situation of failure to one of success. Iraq is an easy target, it is assumed, and a war there will lead the country to rally around Bush as it did after the attacks on September 11.

Is it about oil? I have no doubt that oil is a big factor. All of the U.S. policies in the Middle East since the Second

This interview, conducted by Anthony Arnove, originally appeared in *Socialist Worker* on September 13, 2002. Reprinted, with minor changes, by permission.

World War have been rooted in the desire to control the enormous oil reserves there—and certainly to control the price of oil and the profits from oil.

Oil is not the only reason. There is the political motive of winning popular support by creating a war atmosphere. Then there's the motive of establishing control in a country that has so far eluded the American grasp. The United States cannot abide the existence of nations that do not go along submissively with American policy. Iraq used to be such a country, when it was a close ally, but that changed when Iraq invaded Kuwait in 1990.

Also, a war with Iraq will help maintain the emergency atmosphere in the United States, in which civil liberties are curtailed, for both noncitizens and citizens, with war being the convenient excuse.

ARNOVE: The Bush administration and the other supporters of war justify the "war on terrorism" with rhetoric about democracy. What are their real interests?

ZINN: The real interests of the Bush administration—and the Democratic Party supporters of war—are what the interests of the United States have been for a very long time, long before September 11.

The long-term interest of American governments, from the end of the Revolutionary War to the present day, has been the expansion of national power, first on the continent, then into the Caribbean and the Pacific, and, since the Second World War, everywhere on the globe.

Each time there was a period of expansion, there was an explanation: "Manifest Destiny," the need to "save Spain," the need to "civilize" and bring Christianity to the Filipinos, the Germans are sinking our merchant vessels, North Korea has invaded South Korea, we've been fired on in the Gulf of Tonkin, we need to stop the spread of communism.

But behind all those justifications was the urge to expand American economic and military power. The "war on terrorism" is the latest opportunity to expand U.S. political, economic, and military power into other parts of the world.

ARNOVE: Some people have compared the situation of the detainees from September 11 with the incarceration of Japanese Americans during the Second World War. You lived through that period. What was the climate like?

ZINN: The incarceration of the Japanese took place with the American public unaware or only vaguely aware that it was happening. Many liberals and radicals, knowing what was happening, were silent, believing it was necessary to win the war. Racist attitudes toward the Japanese were widespread in the population, thus making it harder for sympathy to be aroused.

Today, anti-immigration sentiment and racism are still strong in this county. It's disturbing to see that Muslims have been detained without benefit of constitutional rights and with no public outcry.

ARNOVE: As a participant in the civil rights movement, what was it like to hear political leaders talk about saluting the flag and knowing that the most elementary rights supposedly guaranteed under that flag were being denied to African Americans?

ZINN: Black Americans have always been ambivalent toward the flag and "patriotism." On the one hand, they have wanted to be recognized as supporters of the country, as people willing to fight in the nation's wars. On the other hand, they have recognized that wars "for freedom" were based on hypocrisy, given what was happening to blacks in this country.

Blacks in the Civil War struggled for the right to fight in the war and yet knew they were being used as cannon fodder and treated as inferiors. Black soldiers in the Philippines at first welcomed the chance to show that they could serve in the military as whites did, but they soon realized that they were killing people of color while back home their black countrymen were being lynched.

In the Second World War, though certain black leaders (Joe Louis, notably) were used to build up black support for the war, there was a great deal of disaffection, not only because of segregation in the armed forces but also because of how blacks were treated in the nation. Franklin Delano Roosevelt, for instance, refused to support an antilynching bill.

And in the southern civil rights movement, blacks were among the first to declare their opposition to the Vietnam War, pointing out how the federal government, under both John F. Kennedy and Lyndon Johnson, was collaborating with southern racists and was not protecting blacks from violence.

ARNOVE: With the anniversary of September 11 approaching, politicians are again wrapping themselves in the flag and talking about freedom and democracy. What are their motives?

ZINN: The record of American political leaders on "freedom and democracy" is so poor that wrapping themselves in the flag is an attempt to conceal that record.

That record includes the starving of funds for health care, jobs, and housing while huge sums are expended on the military. It also includes the imprisonment of huge numbers of people of color, whose desperate situation growing up is due to the neglect of poor people in this country by our political leaders. Their patriotism is a way of covering all of that over and distracting people from these issues.

ARNOVE: Initially, the Vietnam War had the same level of patriotic support as all the others. But significant numbers of people ultimately turned against it. When did this begin to change and why?

ZINN: There was a dramatic shift in American public opinion between 1965, when 61 percent of those polled supported the war, and 1971, when 61 percent opposed the war.

You saw a gradual buildup of opposition. In 1965, one hundred people gathered on the Boston Common to protest the war. In 1969, one hundred thousand gathered there to protest the war. Later, millions were involved in demonstrations around the country.

I believe the change was due to the fact that the American people, by 1967 and 1968, finally began to understand that it was a brutal war against innocent people. They saw images on television of U.S. Marines burning peasant huts, of children being napalm victims, of the My Lai Massacre. And also, they saw the toll of American lives mounting week by week.

I believe this is an important thing to remember. There is no natural inclination to support war; it has to be artificially induced by political leaders. And when Americans, normally of good will and decent morality, begin to get information different from the official line, they have second thoughts and question the official line.

ARNOVE: Eugene Debs, the leading U.S. socialist at the beginning of the last century, had a lot to say about this question of patriotism. Could you talk about his views of war and patriotism?

ZINN: Debs was a leader in the protest against the First World War. He was sentenced to ten years in prison, a decision that was affirmed by a unanimous Supreme Court led by the presumed liberal jurist Oliver Wendell Holmes. Debs was sentenced because in a speech in Canton, Ohio, he said that the master classes made the wars and the working classes fought in them.

He said: "Wars throughout history have been waged for conquest and plunder. In the Middle Ages, when the feudal lords who inhabited the castles whose towers may still be seen along the Rhine concluded to enlarge their domains, to increase their power, their prestige and their wealth, they declared war upon one another. But they themselves did not go to war, any more than the modern feudal lords, the barons of Wall Street, go to war.

"The feudal barons of the Middle Ages, the economic predecessors of the capitalists of our day, declared all wars. And their miserable serfs fought all the battles. The poor, ignorant serfs had been taught to revere their masters; to believe that when their masters declared war upon one another, it was their patriotic duty to fall upon one another and to cut one another's throats for the profit and glory of the lords and barons who held them in contempt.

"And that is war in a nutshell. The master class has always declared the wars; the subject class has always fought the battles. The master class has had all to gain and nothing to lose, while the subject class has had nothing to gain and all to lose—especially their lives."[1]

Debs rightly saw war in class terms—as benefiting the rich, and killing the poor.

NOTE

1. Jean Y. Tussey, ed., *Eugene V. Debs Speaks* (New York: Pathfinder Press, 1970).

9
THE DIVERTED LEFT

◦

Many people who consider themselves liberal, even radical, seem obsessed with the fear that Clinton's ordeal will loose a wave of sexual McCarthyism on our country. One might think that the sight of the corpses of Iraqi civilians killed during the first Gulf War, American bombings and Clinton's call for more billions for the Pentagon, including a revival of Reagan's Star Wars project, would restore a sense of proportion to those who think the most important issue today is the attack on Clinton rather than Clinton's attacks on the country and the world.

Those on the Left who are outraged over the impeachment/removal proceedings try not to place Clinton himself at the center of their concern. They know they would be hard put to defend his record as president, although some of them are so carried away by indignation over the bigotry of the Right that they occasionally say something like "He's done some good things." Others, aware that his

An earlier version of this essay appeared in *The Progressive* in February 1999. Copyright © 1999 by Howard Zinn. Reprinted with permission.

"good things" could fit into a thimble and his "bad things" are mountainous, are content with the timid disclaimer, as one circulating petition put it, that "the undersigned have different opinions of Clinton."

Those who oppose the impeachment of Clinton say that their concern is not Clinton but the danger posed by right-wing Comstockites who will move on from Clinton to the rest of us; they are concerned that the right to sexual privacy will be imperiled, that prurient puritans will poison the freedoms won by the cultural revolution of recent decades. I would suggest that this is an overheated reaction to a last-ditch attempt of a minority that is loud and powerful, but still a minority, to impose on the people of the country a set of sexual restrictions they have already rejected.

The clear sign of this rejection is the public's repeated refusal, in survey after survey, to repudiate Clinton. This is often explained by his personal "popularity," or by the nation's economic contentment, but it is more likely a statement about the right to privacy, which all Americans want and which they are willing to grant even to a mediocre, charming rascal of a president.

The evidence is quite clear that the public, except for a hard-core minority of the righteous Right, has by and large already accepted the principles of sexual freedom now under attack. The 1960s and 1970s, volatile with the movements of black people, antiwar protesters, and women, provoked a sexual revolution that has changed our culture beyond the possibility of reversal. That revolution is visible in the movies, on television and radio, and in magazines, where there is a clear acceptance, startling to those who recall earlier decades, of gays and lesbians, of nudity, of premarital and extramarital sex (observe the popularity in mainstream America of *The Bridges of Madi-*

son County). This suggests that progressives worried about sexual McCarthyism have organized a safari against a paper tiger. They are off in the jungle to wage a war that has largely been won. And they have deserted a battlefield dominated by Clinton and the Republicans, who have joined, through all the years of his presidency, to act against the poor, to make the corporate rich richer, to maintain an enormous military apparatus, and to use it against helpless people abroad. Clinton's major policies have had Republican support: the destruction of the New Deal's guarantees to poor women and children, the building of more prisons and the extension of capital punishment, the refusal to sign the land mines treaty and to end nuclear testing, the continued sale of weapons all over the world, the cruel punishment by embargo of the Iraqi and Cuban peoples, and the repeated bombing of Iraq that produce civilian casualties. In short, many people on the American Left have been hoodwinked (by themselves) into surrendering their historic mission as critics of the bipartisan Establishment. They are diverting their energies and talents at a time when the voices for economic justice at home and human rights abroad need to be louder than ever.

10
A CAMPAIGN WITHOUT CLASS

There came a rare amusing moment in the 2000 election campaign when George Bush (who had $220 million for his campaign) accused Al Gore (who had only $170 million) of appealing to "class warfare." It recalled the 1988 election campaign when Bush's father (is this a genetic disorder?) accused candidate Michael Dukakis of instigating class antagonism.

I noticed that neither of the accused responded with a defiant acknowledgment that "Yes, we have classes in this country." Only Ralph Nader has dared to suggest that this country is divided among the rich, the poor, and the nervous in between. This kind of talk is considered to be unpardonably rude and would be enough to bar him from the televised debates.

We have learned that we mustn't talk of class divisions in this country. It upsets our political leaders. We must believe that we are one family—me and Exxon, you and

An earlier version of this essay appeared in *The Progressive* in November 2000. Copyright © 2000 by Howard Zinn. Reprinted with permission.

Microsoft, the children of the CEOs and the children of the janitors. Our interests are the same—that's why we speak of going to war "for the national interest" as if it was in all our interests; why we maintain an enormous military budget for "national security," as if our nuclear weapons strengthen the security of all and not the securities of some.

That's why our culture is soaked in the idea of patriotism, which is piped into our consciousness from the first grade, where we begin every day by reciting the Pledge of Allegiance: ". . . one nation, under God, indivisible, with liberty and justice for all." I remember stumbling over that big word *indivisible*—with good reason, although I didn't know the reason, being quite politically backward at the age of six. Only later did I begin to understand that our nation, from the start, has been divided by class, race, and national origin and has been beset by fierce conflicts, yes, class conflicts, throughout its history.

The culture labors strenuously to keep class conflict out of the history books, to maintain the idea of a monolithic, noble "us" against a shadowy but unmistakably evil "them." It starts with the story of the American Revolution, in which, as the 2000 movie *The Patriot* (kindergarten history, put on screen for millions of viewers) told us once more, we were united in glorious struggle against British rule. The mythology surrounding the Founding Fathers is based on the idea that we Americans were indeed one family, and that our founding document, the Constitution, represented all our interests, as declared proudly by the opening words of its preamble—"We, the People of the United States. . . ."

It may therefore seem surly for us to report that the American Revolution was not a war waged by a united population. The one hundred and fifty years leading up to the revolution were filled with conflict, yes, class conflict—servants and slaves against their masters, tenants against landlords, poor people in the cities rioting for food and flour against profiteering merchants, mutinies of sailors against their captains. Thus, when the Revolutionary War began, some colonists saw the war as one of liberation, but many others saw it as the substitution of one set of rulers for another. As for black slaves and Indians, there was little to choose between the British and the Americans.

This class conflict inside the revolution came dramatically alive with mutinies in George Washington's army. In 1781, after enduring five years of war (casualties in the revolution exceeded, in proportion to population, American casualties in World War II), more than one thousand soldiers in the Pennsylvania line at Morristown, New Jersey, mostly foreign-born from Ireland, Scotland, and Germany, mutinied. They had seen their officers paid handsomely and fed and clothed well while the privates and sergeants were fed slop, marched in rags without shoes, and paid in virtually worthless Continental currency or not paid at all for months. They were abused, beaten, and whipped by their officers for the smallest breach of discipline.

The mutineers' deepest grievance was that they wanted out of the war, claiming their terms of enlistment had expired and that they were kept in the army by force. They were aware that in the spring of 1780 eleven deserters of the Connecticut line in Morristown had been sentenced to death, but at the last minute those mutineers had received a reprieve, except for one of them, who had forged discharges for a hundred men. He was hanged.

General Washington, facing by this time 1,700 mutineers (a substantial part of his army) assembled at Princeton, New Jersey, decided to make concessions. Many of the rebels were allowed to leave the army, and Washington asked the governors of the various states for money to deal with the grievances of the soldiers. The Pennsylvania line quieted down. But when another mutiny broke out in the New Jersey line, involving only a few hundred, Washington ordered harsh measures. He saw the possibility of "this dangerous spirit" spreading. Two of "the most atrocious offenders" were court-martialed on the spot and sentenced to be shot, and their fellow mutineers, some of them weeping as they did so, carried out the executions.

In the novel *The Proud and the Free,* Howard Fast tells the story of these mutinies, drawing from the classic historical account by Carl Van Doren, *Mutiny in January.* Fast dramatizes the class conflict inside the Revolutionary Army as one of his characters, the mutinous soldier Jack Maloney, recalls the words of Thomas Paine and the promise of freedom and says, yes, he is willing to die for that freedom, but "not for that craven Congress in Philadelphia, not for the fine Pennsylvania ladies in their silks and satins, not for the property of every dirty lord and fat patroon in New Jersey."

When the War for Independence was won, class conflict continued in the new nation, as the Founding Fathers fashioned a constitution that would enable a strong federal government to suppress any rebellion by their unruly children. The new government would serve the interests of slaveholders, merchants, manufacturers, and land speculators while offering white males with some property a degree of influence, but not dominance, in the political process.

The history of the following two hundred years is a history of control of the nation by one class, as the government, solidly in the hands of the rich, gave huge gifts of the nation's resources to railroad magnates, manufacturers, and shipowners. Charles Beard, in the first years of the Great Depression, wrote caustically about "The Myth of Rugged Individualism," noting that industrial and financial leaders were not rugged enough to make their own way in the world and had to be subsidized, and fed with silver spoons, by the government.

When the ruling class (I've tried to avoid that old-fashioned radical expression, but it expresses a simple, strong truth) faced resistance, as they did all through the nineteenth and twentieth centuries, from slaves, working people, farmers, and especially by the indigenous people of the continent, they called upon the government to use its armies and its courts to put down the ingrates.

Political leaders, then and now, would become especially annoyed when someone dared to suggest that we live in a class society dominated by the moneyed interests. Thus, when Eugene Debs, opposing World War I, told an assembly in Ohio that "the master class has always brought a war, and the subject class has always fought the battle," this could not be tolerated. He was sentenced to ten years in prison, and Oliver Wendell Holmes, in the spirit of patriotic liberalism, affirmed the sentence for a unanimous Supreme Court.

Even the slightest suggestion that we are a nation divided by class brings angry reactions. All Al Gore had to do in 2000 was to talk ominously about "big money" (while pocketing huge amounts of it for his campaign) for George Bush to become indignant. Surely Bush did not need to worry. Gore and Joseph Lieberman represented no threat to the rule of the super-rich. The *New York Times* hastened to reassure Bush; a front-page story in August 2000 was headlined "As a Senator, Lieberman Is Proudly Pro-Business" and went on to give the comforting details: that the Silicon Valley high-tech industry loves Lieberman, that the military–industrial complex of Connecticut was grateful to him for making sure it got $7.5 billion in contracts for the Sea Wolf submarine.

The unity of both major parties around class issues (despite rhetoric and posturing by the Democrats to win the support of organized labor) becomes most clear when you see the total disaffection from politics of people at the bottom of the economic ladder. A *New York Times* reporter, in a rare excursion into "the other America," spoke to people in Cross City, Florida, about the 2000 election and concluded, "People here look at Al Gore and George W. Bush and see two men born to the country club, men whose family histories jingle with silver spoons. They appear, to people here, just the same."

Cindy Lamb, a cashier at a Chevron filling station and the wife of a construction worker, told the reporter, "I don't think they think about people like us, and if they do care, they're not going to do anything for us. Maybe if they had ever lived in a two bedroom trailer, it would be different." An African American woman, a manager at McDonald's who made slightly more than the minimum wage of $5.15 an hour, said about Bush and Gore, "I don't even pay attention to those two, and all my friends say the same. My life won't change."

That election is over, and now we're faced with a similar choice in 2004, between George W. Bush and John Kerry, another Democrat appealing to the middle and working classes while maintaining his ties to the wealthy interests of the nation and supporting the bipartisan imperial policy. Whether Bush or Kerry wins the 2004 election, the same class that has always dominated our political and economic systems will be in power. Whoever is president, we will face the same challenge the day after the inauguration: how to bring together the class of the have-nots—a great majority of the country—into the kind of social movement that in the past has made the people in charge tremble at the prospect of "class warfare" and has gained some measure of justice.

Such a movement, responding to the great challenges of the new century, could bring democracy alive.

11
FEDERAL BUREAU OF INTIMIDATION

᠊ᢒ᠊

I thought it would be good to talk about the FBI because
they talk about us. They don't like to be talked about.
They don't even like the fact that you're listening to them
being talked about. They are very sensitive people. If you
look into the history of the FBI and Martin Luther King—
which now has become notorious in that totally notorious
history of the FBI— the FBI attempted to neutralize him,
perhaps kill him, perhaps get him to commit suicide, certainly to destroy him as a leader of black people in the
United States. And if you follow the progression of that
treatment of King, it starts not with the Montgomery Bus
Boycott but when King begins to criticize the FBI. You
see, then Hoover's ears, all four of them, suddenly perk
up. And he says, okay, we have to start working on King.

I was interested in this especially because I was reading the Church Committee report. In 1975, the Senate
Select Committee investigated the CIA and the FBI, issued

An earlier form of this essay was given as a talk at the Community
Church in Boston in October 1992.

voluminous reports, and pointed out at what point the FBI became interested in King. In 1961–1962, after the Montgomery Bus Boycott, after the sit-ins, after the Freedom Rides of '61, there was an outbreak of mass demonstrations in a very little, very southern, almost slave town of southern Georgia called Albany. There had been nothing like this in that town. This was a quiet, apparently passive, town, and everybody was happy, of course. And then suddenly the black people rose up, and a good part of the black population of Albany ended up in jail. There were not enough jails for all who demonstrated.

A report was made for the Southern Regional Council of Atlanta on the events in Albany. The report, which was very critical of the FBI, came out in the *New York Times*. And King was asked what he thought of the role of the FBI. He said he agreed with the report that the FBI was not doing its job, that the FBI was racist, et cetera, et cetera.

At that point, the FBI also inquired who the author of that report was and asked that an investigation begin on the author. Since I had written it, I was interested in the FBI's interest in the author. In fact, through the Freedom of Information Act, I sent away for whatever information the FBI had on me. I became curious, I guess. I wanted to test myself, because if I found that the FBI did not have a dossier on me it would have been tremendously embarrassing and I wouldn't have been able to face my friends. But, fortunately, there were several hundred pages of absolutely inconsequential material. Very consequential for the FBI, I suppose, but inconsequential for any intelligent person.

I'm talking about the FBI and U.S. democracy because here we have this peculiar situation that we live in a democratic country—everybody knows that, everybody says it, it's repeated, it's dinned into our ears a thousand times, you grow up, you pledge allegiance, you salute the flag, you hail democracy, you look at the totalitarian states, you read the history of tyrannies, and here is the beacon light of democracy. And, of course, there's some truth to that. There are things you can do in the United States that you can't do many other places without being put in jail.

But the United States is a very complex system. It's very hard to describe because, yes, there are elements of democracy; there are things that you're grateful for, such as that you're not in front of the death squads in El Salvador. On the other hand, it's not quite a democracy. And one of the things that makes it not quite a democracy is the existence of outfits like the FBI and the CIA. Democracy is based on openness, and the existence of a secret policy, or of secret lists of dissident citizens, violates the spirit of democracy. There are a lot of other things that make the United States less than a democracy. For instance, what happens in police stations and in the encounters between police and citizens on the street. Or what happens in the military, which is a kind of fascist enclave inside this democracy. Or what happens in courtrooms, which are supposedly little repositories of democracy but are presided over by "emperors" who decide everything that happens in a courtroom—what evidence is given, what evidence is withheld, what instructions are given to the jury, what sentences are ultimately meted out to the guilty, and so on.

So it's a peculiar kind of democracy. Yes, you vote. You have a choice. Clinton, Bush, and Perot! It's fantastic. *Time* and *Newsweek*. CBS and NBC. It's called a pluralist society. But in so many of the little places of everyday life in which life is lived out, somehow democracy doesn't exist. And one of the creeping hands of totalitarianism running through the democracy is the Federal Bureau of Investigation.

I think it was seeing the film *Mississippi Burning* that led me to want to talk about the FBI. I had sort of reached a point where I said, "Who wants to hear any more about the FBI?" But then I saw *Mississippi Burning*. It relates a very, very important incident in the history of the civil rights movement in the United States. In the summer of 1964, three young men in the movement, two white and one black, had traveled to investigate the burning of a church in a place called Philadelphia, Mississippi—city of brotherly love. They were arrested, held in jail, released in the night, followed by cars, stalked, beaten very, very badly with chains and clubs, and shot to death—executed—on June 21, 1964. Their bodies were found in August. It's a great theme for an important film.

Mississippi Burning, I suppose, does something useful in capturing the terror of Mississippi, the violence, the ugliness. But after the film does that, it does something that I think is very harmful: In showing the apprehension of the murderers, it portrays two FBI operatives and a whole flotilla—if FBI men float—of FBI people as the heroes of this episode. Anybody who knows anything about the history of the civil rights movement, or certainly people who were in the movement at that time in the South, would have to be horrified by that portrayal. I was just one of many people who were involved in the movement. I was teaching in Atlanta, Georgia, in a black college for about seven years from 1956 to 1963, and I became involved in the movement in Albany, Georgia, and Selma, Alabama, and Hattiesburg, Mississippi, and Greenwood, Greenville, and Jackson, Mississippi in the summer of 1964. I was involved with SNCC, the Student Nonviolent Coordinating Committee. Anybody who was involved in the southern movement at that time knew with absolute certainty that the FBI could not be counted on and was not the friend of the civil rights movement.

The FBI stood by with their suits and ties and took notes while people were being beaten in front of them. This happened again, and again, and again. The Justice Department, to which the FBI is presumably accountable, was called again and again in times of stress by people of the civil rights movement saying, hey, somebody's in danger here. Somebody's about to be beaten, somebody's about to be arrested, somebody's about to be killed. We need help from the federal government. We do have a constitution, don't we? We do have rights. We do have the constitutional right to just live, or to walk, or to speak, or to pray, or to demonstrate. We have the Bill of Rights. It's America. It's a democracy. You're the Justice Department, your job is to enforce the Constitution of the United States. That's what you took an oath to do, so where are you? The Justice Department wasn't responding. They wouldn't return phone calls, they wouldn't show up, or when they did show up, they did nothing.

The civil rights movement was very, very clear about the role of the FBI. And it wasn't just the FBI; it goes back to the Justice Department; back to Washington; back to politics; back to Kennedy appointing racist judges in Alabama, Mississippi, and Georgia to do favors for his southern Democratic political cronies and only becoming concerned about black people when things appeared on television that embarrassed the administration and the nation before the world.

Only then did things happen. Oh, we'll send troops to Little Rock, we'll send troops to Oxford, Mississippi, and so on. Do something big and dramatic. But in all the days and all the hours in between, before and after, if there's no

international attention, forget it. Leave these black folks at
the mercy of the law enforcement officers down there, just
as after the Civil War blacks were left at the mercy of
southern power and southern plantation owners by north-
ern politicians who made their deal with the white South
in 1877.

If you want to read the hour-by-hour description of
this, you could read a wonderful book by Mary King,
Freedom Song. She was a SNCC staff person in the Atlanta
office whose job was to get on the phone and call the
newspapers, the government, the Justice Department and
say, Hey, three young men have not come back from Philadelphia, Mississippi. She called and called and called, and
it took several days before she got a response. They were
dead. Probably none of those calls would have saved them.

It was too late, but there was something that could have
saved them, and it's something I haven't seen reported in
the press. If there had been federal agents accompanying
the three on their trip, if there had been federal agents in
the police station in Philadelphia, Mississippi, that might
not have happened. If there had been somebody determined to the enforce law, enforce constitutional rights,
protect the rights of people who were just going around,
driving, talking, working, then those three murders might
have been averted.

In fact, twelve days before the three men disappeared
there was a gathering in Washington, D.C., on June 9,
1964. A busload of black Mississippians came all the way
up—it was a long bus ride to Washington—to the National Theater.

There was a jury of fairly well-known Americans—college presidents, writers, other people—assembled to hear
the black people's testimony before the press, and an au-
dience was recorded and transcribed. They testified that

what was going to happen in Mississippi that summer with all these volunteers coming down was very, very dangerous. They testified about their experiences, about their history of being beaten, about the bodies of black people found floating in the rivers of Mississippi, and they said, People are going to get killed; we need the protection of the federal government.

Also appearing at this hearing were specialists in constitutional law who made the proper legal points that the federal government had absolute power to protect people going down into Mississippi. Section 333, Title 10 of the U.S. Code (some numbers burn themselves into you because you have to use them again and again) gives the federal government the power to do anything to enforce constitutional rights when local authorities either refuse or fail to protect those rights.

So they take all this testimony at the National Theater, put it into a transcript, and deliver it to Attorney General Robert Kennedy, hand deliver it to the White House, and ask the federal government to send marshals down to Mississippi. Not an army, just a few hundred marshals in plain clothes. This is 1964; by now you've sent forty thousand soldiers to Vietnam, so you can send two hundred plainclothes officers to Mississippi. No response from the attorney general, none from the president. Twelve days later those three men disappear.

Well, why didn't they put that in the film? Why didn't anybody say anything about that? So the FBI agents are the heroes of this film.

Well, that's only part, as you know, of the history of the FBI. Going back, the FBI was formed first as the Bureau of Investigation under Theodore Roosevelt—don't worry, I'm not going to take you year by year through this history. It's a very depressing history. In 1908, Theodore

Roosevelt's attorney general, a man named Bonaparte, a grandnephew of Napoleon, set up the Bureau of Investigation, which later became the FBI. One of its first acts was to enforce a new federal law, the Mann Act. This law made it illegal to transport women across state lines for immoral purposes. One of their first acts was to prosecute black heavyweight champion Jack Johnson, because he was living with a white woman and they actually crossed a state line. This was one of the first heroic acts of the FBI.

Racism goes way back in the FBI and comes way forward, comes right up to the present. By the way—*Mississippi Burning* shows a black FBI agent. But there was no black person in the FBI in 1964. A chauffeur, maybe. A maid, maybe. But no black FBI agents in 1964. Yes, the racism comes right up to yesterday [October 1992] when a black FBI man—in Detroit, I think—is harassed by his fellow white FBI agents, who do all sorts of funny things to him to make his life miserable. You think, where is the solidarity among FBI people? FBI people, black and white together, we shall overcome. Well, apparently the FBI doesn't believe in that.

There's too much to say about the FBI and racism. It's not just J. Edgar Hoover. Everybody says, oh, J. Edgar Hoover, he really hated black people. He hated the civil rights movement, but it's not just him, of course. It's too easy to pin all this on J. Edgar Hoover, to pin it on just the FBI as if they're wild cards. The president says, oh, sorry, we didn't know what they were doing. Well, it's just like Oliver North. A wild card North was doing these crazy things, and his defense was absolutely right: I did it for them. He did. He did it for them, and now they have turned on him. He doesn't have to worry, they'll take good care of him. They take care of their own.

When people in the CIA and FBI commit crimes, how do they get handled? They don't. They're forgotten about.

Do you know how many crimes have been committed by the FBI and the CIA? How many black bag jobs? Breaking and entering? Try breaking and entering. Really. Try breaking and entering in the daytime, or nighttime, and see what happens to you. Different punishments depending on what hour of the day. The FBI broke and entered again and again, hundreds and hundreds of times.

There were hundreds of FBI men involved in these break-ins. Two men were actually prosecuted. This happens every once in a while. When huge public attention finally gets focused on the misdeeds of the FBI, they pick out two from the pack, prosecute them, find them guilty, and sentence them. To what? To nothing. A fine, $5,000 for one person and $3,500 for the other. That's FBI petty cash. And then they say that justice has been done and the system works.

Remember when Richard Helms of the CIA was found guilty of perjury in 1976? In 1950, Alger Hiss went to jail for four years for perjury; Helms didn't go to jail for two hours. And Helms's perjury, if you examine it, was far, far more serious than Hiss's, if Hiss was indeed guilty. But if you're CIA, if you're FBI, you get off.

But Oliver North is right; he did it for them. He did what they expected him, wanted him, to do. They use this phrase, plausible denial—a very neat device. You have to be able to do things that the president wants you to do but that he can deny he wanted you to do or deny he ordered you to do if push comes to shove.

It's not just the FBI. It's the government. It's part of the system, not just a few people here and there. The FBI has the names of millions of people. The FBI has a security index of tens of thousands of people— they won't tell us the exact numbers. Security index. That's people who in the event of national emergency will be picked up without trial and held. Just like that. The FBI has been preparing for a long time, waiting for an emergency. You get horrified at South Africa, or Israel, or Haiti, where they detain people without trial, just pick them up and hold them incommunicado. You never hear from them, don't know where they are. The FBI has been preparing to do this for a long time. Just waiting for an emergency. These are all countries in emergency; South Africa's in an emergency, Chile was in an emergency.

James Madison made the point way back. The Founding Fathers were not dumb. They may have been rich, and white, and reactionary, and slaveholders, but they weren't dumb. Madison said the best way to infringe on liberty is to create an external menace.

What can a citizen do in a situation like this? Well, one thing is simply to expose the FBI. They hate to be exposed; they're a secret outfit. Everything they do is secret. Their threat rests on secrecy. We don't know where they are, who they are, or what they're doing. Are they tapping your phone? Right. And what are you going to do about it? The one thing you shouldn't think will do anything is passing a law against the FBI. There are always people who come up with that. That's the biggest laugh in the world. These are people who pay absolutely no attention to the law, again and again. They've violated the law thousands of times. Pass another law; that's funny.

No, the only thing you can do with the FBI is expose them to public understanding—education, ridicule. They deserve it. They have "garbologists" ransacking garbage pails (there's a lot of interesting stuff in garbage pails). They have to be exposed, brought down from that hallowed point where they once were. And, by the way, they have been brought down. That's one of the comforting things about what has happened in the United States in the past thirty years. The FBI at one point was absolutely untouchable. Everybody had great respect for the FBI. In 1965, when a poll asked Americans "Do you have a strong admiration for the FBI?" 85 percent of respondents answered "yes." When they asked again in 1975, 35 percent said "yes." That's a big comedown. That's education—education by events, education by exposure. The FBI knows it has come down in the public mind and so now it's trying to look kinder and gentler. But they're not likely to merge with the American Civil Liberties Union. They're more likely, whatever their soothing words, to keep doing what they're in the habit of doing, assaulting the rights of citizens.

The most important thing you can do is simply to continue exposing the FBI. Because why does the FBI do all this? To scare the hell out of people. Were they doing this because of a Soviet invasion threat or because they thought the Socialist Workers Party was about to take over the country? Are they going after whoever their current target is because the country is in imminent danger, internal or external? No. They are doing it because they don't like these organizations. They don't like the civil rights organizations, they don't like the women's organizations, they don't like the antiwar organizations, they don't like the Central American organizations. They don't like social movements. They work for the establishment, and the corporations, and the politicos to keep things as they are. And they want to frighten and chill the people who are trying to change things. So the best defense against and resistance against them is simply to keep on fighting back, to keep on exposing them. That's all I have to say.

12
WHY STUDENTS SHOULD STUDY HISTORY: AN INTERVIEW

৯

MINER: Why should students study history?

ZINN: I started studying history with one view in mind: to look for answers to the issues and problems I saw in the world about me. By the time I went to college I had worked in a shipyard, had been in the Air Force, had been in a war. I came to history asking questions about war and peace, about wealth and poverty, about racial division.

Sure, there's a certain interest in inspecting the past, and it can be fun, sort of like a detective story. I can make an argument for knowledge for its own sake as something that can add to your life. But while that's good, it is small in relation to the very large objective of trying to understand and do something about the issues that face us in the world today.

The following is condensed from an interview with Barbara Miner that appeared in *Rethinking Our Classrooms: Teaching for Equity and Justice,* vol. 1, ed. Bill Bigelow, Linda Christensen, Stan Karp, Barbara Miner, and Bob Peterson (Rethinking Schools: Milwaukee, 1994), 150–53. Used by permission of Howard Zinn and Rethinking Schools.

Students should be encouraged to go into history in order to come out of it, and they should be discouraged from going into history and getting lost in it, as some historians do.

MINER: What do you see as some of the major problems in how U.S. history has been taught in this country?

ZINN: One major problem has been the intense focus on U.S. history in isolation from the world. This is a problem that all nations have, their nationalistic focus on their own history, and it goes to absurd lengths. Some states in this country even require a yearlong course in the history of that state.

But even if you are willing to see the United States in relation to world history, you face the problem that we have not looked at the world in an equitable way. We have concentrated on the Western world, in fact on western Europe. I remember coming into my first class in Spelman College in Atlanta in 1956 and finding that there was no required course in black history, or Asian or African history, but there was a required course in the history of England. And there on the board was this chart of the Tudors and the Stuarts, the dynasties of England.

For the United States, lack of emphasis has been particularly glaring in terms of Latin America, which is that part of the world closest to us and with which we've had the most to do economically and politically.

Another glaring problem has been the emphasis in teaching American history through the eyes of the important and powerful people, through the presidents, the Congress, the Supreme Court, the generals, the industrialists. History textbooks don't say, "We are going to tell the story of the Mexican War from the standpoint of the generals," but when they tell us it was a great military victory, that's exactly what they are doing. Taking that as an example, if one were to have a more inclusive view of the war with Mexico, what would be some of the themes and perspectives one would include?

The Mexican War is an example of how one event raises so many issues. You'd have to see the war first of all as more than a military action. So often the history of war is dominated by the story of battles, and this is a way of diverting attention from the political factors behind a war. It's possible to concentrate upon the battles of the Mexican War and to talk just about the triumphant march into Mexico City and not about the relationship of the Mexican War to slavery and to the acquisition of territories that might possibly be slave territories.

Another thing that is neglected in the history of the Mexican War is the viewpoint of the ordinary soldiers. The soldiers who had volunteered for the Mexican War—you didn't need a draft because so many people in the working classes were so destitute that they would join the military on the promise of a little bit of pay and mustering out money and a little bit of prestige—went into it not really knowing the bloodshed it would involve. And then so many of them deserted. For example, seven regiments of General Winfield Scott deserted on the road to Mexico City.

You should tell the story of the Massachusetts volunteers who went into the Mexican War. Half of them died, and the half who returned were invited to a homecoming party, and when a commanding officer got up to address the gathering, they booed him off the platform.

I think it's a good idea also to do something that isn't done anywhere so far as I know in histories in any country, and that is: tell the story of the war from the standpoint of the other side, of "the enemy." To tell the story of the

Mexican War from the standpoint of the Mexicans means to ask: How did they feel about having 40 percent of their territory taken away from them as a result of the war? How did they view the incident that President Polk used as a reason for the beginning of the war? Did it look real or manufactured to them? You'd also have to talk about the people in the United States who protested against the war. That would be the time to bring up Henry Thoreau and his essay "Civil Disobedience." You'd have to look at Congress and how it behaved. You'd have to look at Abraham Lincoln, who was in the House of Representatives during the Mexican War. You'd learn a lot about politicians and politics, because you'd see that Abraham Lincoln on the one hand spoke up against the war but on the other hand voted to give money to finance the war. This is so important because this is something that is repeated again and again in American history: the feeble opposition in Congress to presidential wars and then the voting of funds for whatever war the president has initiated.

MINER: How do you prevent history lessons from becoming a recitation of dates and battles and congresspersons and presidents?

ZINN: You can take any incident in American history and enrich it and find parallels with today. One important thing is not to concentrate on chronological order but to go back and forth and find similarities and analogies.

You should ask students if anything in a particular historical event reminds them of something they read in the newspapers or see on television about the world today. When you press students to make connections, to abstract from the uniqueness of a particular historical event and find something it has in common with another event, then history becomes alive, not just past but present.

And, of course, you must raise the controversial questions and ask students, "Was it *right* for us to take Mexican territory? Should we be proud of that, should we celebrate that?" History teachers often think they must avoid judgments of right and wrong because, after all, those are matters of subjective opinions, those are issues on which students will disagree and teachers will disagree.

But it's the areas of disagreement that are the most important. Questions of right and wrong and justice are exactly the questions that should be raised all the time. When students are asked, "Is this right, is this wrong?" then it becomes interesting, then they can have a debate especially if they learn that there's no simple, absolute, agreed upon, universal answer. It's not like giving them multiple-choice questions where they are right or wrong. I think that's a tremendous advance in their understanding of what education is.

Teachers must also address the problem that people have been miseducated to become dependent on government, to think that their supreme act as citizens is to go to the polls and vote every two years or four years. That's where the history of social movements comes in. Teachers should dwell on Shays' Rebellion, on colonial rebellions, on the abolitionist movement, on the populist movement, on the labor movement, and so on, and make sure these social movements don't get lost in the overall story of presidents, and Congresses, and Supreme Courts. Emphasizing social and protest movements in the making of history gives students a feeling that they as citizens are the most important actors in history.

Students, for example, should learn that during the Depression there were strikes and demonstrations all over the country. And it was that turmoil and protest that created the atmosphere in which Roosevelt and Congress passed Social Security, unemployment insurance, housing subsidies, and so on.

MINER: How can teachers foster critical thinking so that students don't merely memorize a new, albeit more progressive, set of facts?

ZINN: Substituting one indoctrination for another is a danger, and it's very hard to deal with. After all, the teacher, no matter how hard she or he tries, is the dominant figure in the classroom and has the power of authority and of grades. It's easy for the teacher to fall into the trap of bullying students into accepting one set of facts or ideas. It takes hard work and delicate dealings with students to overcome that. The way I've tried to deal with that problem is to make it clear to the students that when we study history we are dealing with controversial issues with no one, absolute, godlike answer, and that I, as a teacher, have my opinion, and they can have their opinions, and that I, as a teacher, will try to present as much information as I can but that I may leave out information. I try to make them understand that while there are experts on facts, on little things, on the big issues, on the controversies and the issues of right and wrong and justice, there are no experts, and their opinions are as good as mine.

MINER: But how do you then foster a sense of justice and avoid the trap of relativity that, "Well, some people say this and some people say that"?

ZINN: I find such relativity especially true on the college level, where there's a great tendency to indecisiveness. People are unwilling to take a stand on a moral issue because, well, there's this side and there's that side.

I deal with this by example. I never simply present both sides and leave it at that. I take a stand. If I'm dealing with

Columbus, I say, look, there are these people who say that we shouldn't judge Columbus by the standards of the twentieth century. But my view is that basic moral standards are not different for the twentieth century or the fifteenth century. I don't simply lay history out on a platter and say, "I don't care what you choose, they're both valid." I let them know, "No, I care what you choose; I don't think they're both valid. But you don't have to agree with me." I want them to know that if people don't take a stand, the world will remain unchanged, and who wants that?

MINER: Are there specific ways that teachers can foster an antiracist perspective?

ZINN: To a great extent, this moral objective is not considered in teaching history. I think people have to be given the facts of slavery, the facts of racial segregation, the facts of government complicity in racial segregation, the facts of the fight for equality. But that is not enough. I think students need to be aroused emotionally on the issue of equality. They have to try to feel what it was like to be a slave, to be jammed into slave ships, to be separated from your family. Novels, poems, autobiographies, memoirs, the reminiscences of ex-slaves, the letters that slaves wrote, the writings of Frederick Douglass—I think they have to be introduced as much as possible. Students should learn the words of people themselves, to feel their anger, their indignation. In general, I don't think there has been enough use of literature in history. People should read Richard Wright's *Black Boy;* they should read the poems of Countee Cullen; they should read the novels of Alice Walker, the poems of Langston Hughes, Lorraine Hansbury's *A Raisin in the Sun.* These writings have an emotional impact that can't be found in an ordinary recitation of history.

It is especially important that students learn about the relationship of the U.S. government to slavery and race. It's very easy to fall into the view that slavery and racial segregation were a southern problem. The federal government is very often exempted from responsibility for the problem and is presented as a benign force helping black people on the road to equality. In our time, students are taught how Eisenhower sent his troops to Little Rock, Arkansas, and Kennedy sent troops to Oxford, Mississippi, and Congress passed civil rights laws. Yet the federal government is very often an obstacle to resolving those problems of race, and when it enters it comes in late in the picture. Abraham Lincoln was not the initiator of the movement against slavery but a follower of a movement that had developed for thirty years by the time he became president in 1860; it was the antislavery movement that was the major force creating the atmosphere in which emancipation took place following the Civil War. And it was the president and Congress and the Supreme Court that ignored the 13th, 14th, and 15th Amendments after they were passed. In the 1960s it wasn't Johnson and Kennedy who were the leaders and initiators of the movement for race equality, it was black people.

MINER: In addition to focusing on social movements and having a more consciously antiracist perspective, what are some other thematic ways in which the teaching of history must change?

ZINN: I think the issue of class and class conflict needs to be addressed more honestly because it is ignored in traditional nationalist history. This is true not just of the United States but of other countries. Nationhood is a cover for extreme conflicts among classes in society, in our country, from its founding, from the making of the Constitution.

Too often there's a tendency to overlook these conflicts and concentrate on the creation of a national identity.

MINER: How does a teacher deal with the intersection of race, class, and gender in terms of U.S. history, in particular that the white working class has often been complicit, consciously or unconsciously, in some *very* unforgivable actions?

ZINN: The complicity of poor white people in racism, or the complicity of males in sexism, is a very important issue. It seems to me that complicity can't be understood without showing the intense hardships that poor white people faced in this country, making it easier for them to look for scapegoats for their condition. You have to recognize the problems of white working people in order to understand why they turn racist, because they aren't born racist.

When discussing the Civil War, teachers should point out that only a small percentage of the white population of the South owned slaves. The rest of the white population was poor, and they were driven to support slavery and to be racist by the messages of those who controlled society that they would be better off if the Negroes were put in a lower position and that those calling for black equality were threatening the lives of these ordinary white people.

In the history of labor struggles, you should show how blacks and whites were used against one another, how white workers would go out on strike and then black people, desperate themselves for jobs, would be brought in to replace the white workers, how all-white craft unions excluded black workers, and how all this created murderously intense racial antagonisms. So the class and race issues are very much intertwined, as is the gender issue.

One of the ways of giving some satisfaction to men who are themselves exploited is to make them masters in their own households So they may be humiliated on the job, but they come back home and humiliate their wives and their children. There's a wonderful short story by black writer Ann Petry, "Like a Winding Sheet," that should be required reading in school. It's about a black man who is humiliated on the job and comes home and, for the flimsiest of reasons, beats his wife. The story is told in such a way as to make you really understand the pent-up anger that explodes inside a family as a result of what happens out in the world. In all these instances of racial and sexual mistreatment, it is important for students to understand that the roots of such hostility are social, environmental, and situational and are not an inevitability of human nature. It is also important to show how these antagonisms so divide people from one another as to make it difficult for them to solve their common problems in united action.

MINER: How can we explain the roots of this complicity in racism and sexism by white working-class people without falling into the trap of condoning it?

ZINN: That's always a problem: how do you explain something without justifying it? That issue, as a theoretical issue, needs to be explained because it's a common confusion. You need to make the point again and again that trying to understand why people do something is not the same as justifying it. And you need to give specific historical examples of that problem or, as I suggested, literary examples.

MINER: How can you teach white students to take an antiracist perspective that isn't based merely on guilt over the things that white people have done to people of color?

ZINN: If such a perspective is based only on guilt, it doesn't have a secure foundation. It has to be based on empathy and on self-interest, on an understanding that the divisions between black and white have not just resulted in the exploitation of black people, even though they've been the greatest victims, but have prevented whites and blacks from getting together to bring about the social change that would benefit them all. Showing the self-interest is also important in order to avoid the patronizing view of feeling sorry for someone, of giving somebody equality because you feel guilty about what has been done to them.

At the same time, to approach the issue merely on the basis of self-interest would be wrong, because people should learn to empathize with other people even where there is no visible, immediate self-interest.

MINER: In response to concerns about multiculturalism, there's more lip service to include events and perspectives affecting women and people of color. But often it's presented as more facts and people to learn, without any fundamental change in perspective. What would be the approach of a truly antiracist, multicultural perspective in U.S. history?

ZINN: I've noticed this problem in some of the new textbooks, which are obviously trying to respond to the need for a multicultural approach. What I find is a bland eclecticism where everything has equal weight. You add more facts, you add more continents, you add more cultures, you add more people. But then it becomes a confusing mélange in which you've added a lot of different elements but without any real emphasis on what had previously been omitted. You're left with a kind of unemotional, cold combination salad.

You need the equivalent of affirmative action in education. What affirmative action does is to say, look, things have been slanted one way for a long time. We're going to pay special attention to this person or to this group of people because they have been left out for so long. People ask me why in my book *A People's History of the United States* I did not simply add the things that I put in to the orthodox approaches so, as they put it, the book would be better balanced. But there's a way in which this so-called balance leaves people nowhere, with no moral sensibility, no firm convictions, no outrage, no indignation, no energy to go anywhere.

I think it is important to pay special attention to the history of black people, of Indians, and of women in a way that highlights not only the facts but also the emotional intensity of such issues.

MINER: Is it possible for history to be objective?

ZINN: Objectivity is neither possible nor desirable.

It's not possible because all history is subjective; all history represents a point of view. History is always a selection from an infinite number of facts, and everybody makes the selection differently, based on their values and what they think is important. Since it's not possible to be objective, you should be honest about that.

Objectivity is not desirable because if we want to have an effect on the world, we need to emphasize those things that will make students more active citizens and more moral people.

MINER: One of the problems for high school history teachers is they may have five periods and 30 kids in each class, and before you know it they're dealing with 150 students. What types of projects and approaches can they use?

ZINN: The most important thing is to get students to do independent reading and research. Tell the students, "Pick something that interests you, pick out a person who interests you." Your job as teacher is to present them with a wide spectrum of events and people, not just the usual heroes of history but all sorts of people or incidents that they may never have heard of but that might intrigue them. I find that when students have a research project of their own they can get excited about it, especially if they are allowed to choose from a complex set of possibilities.

MINER: How can a progressive teacher promote a radical perspective within a bureaucratic, conservative institution? Teachers sometimes either push the limits so far that they alienate their colleagues or get fired or they're so afraid that they tone down what they really think. How can a teacher resolve this dilemma?

ZINN: The problem certainly exists on the college and university level—people want to get tenure, they want to keep teaching, they want to get promoted, they want to get salary raises, and so there are all these economic punishments if they do something that looks outlandish and radical and different. But I've always believed that the main problem with college and university teachers has been self-censorship. I suspect that the same thing is true in the high schools, although you have to be more sympathetic with high school teachers because they operate in a much more repressive atmosphere. I've seen again and again where college and university teachers don't really have a problem in, for instance, using my *People's History* in their classrooms, but high school teachers always have a problem. They can't get it officially adopted, they have to get permission, they have to photocopy parts of it themselves in order to pass it out to the students, they have to worry about parents complaining, about what the head of the department or the principal or the school superintendent will say.

But I still believe, based on a lot of contact with high school teachers over the past few years, that while there's a danger of becoming overly assertive and insensitive to how others might view you, the most common behavior is timidity. Teachers withdraw and use the real fact of outside control as an excuse for teaching in the orthodox way.

Teachers need to take risks. The problem is how to minimize those risks. One important way is to make sure that you present material in class making it clear that it is subjective, that it is controversial, that you are not laying down the law for students. Another important thing is to be extremely tolerant of students who disagree with your views or students who express racist or sexist ideas. I don't mean tolerant in the sense of not challenging such ideas, but tolerant in the sense of treating them as human beings. It's important to develop a reputation that you don't give kids poor grades on the basis of their disagreements with you. You need to create an atmosphere of freedom in the classroom.

It's also important to talk with other teachers to gain support and encouragement, to organize. Where there are teachers unions, those are logical places for teachers to support and defend one another. Where there are not teachers unions, teachers should always think how they can organize and create a collective strength.

MINER: Teachers don't always know where to get those other perspectives. Do you have any tips?

ZINN: The orthodox perspective is easy to get. But once teachers begin to look for other perspectives, once they start out on that road, they will quickly be led from one thing to another to another.

MINER: So it's not as daunting as people might think?

ZINN: No. It's all there. It's in the library.

INDEX

ABOUT THE AUTHORS

Howard Zinn, professor emeritus of history, Boston University, is the author of *The People's History of the United States* and many other books. He is the author most recently of *The People Speak: American Voices, Some Famous, Some Little Known* (Perennial 2004). He lives in Auburndale, near Boston.

Donaldo Macedo is distinguished professor of liberal arts at the University of Massachusetts Boston. He is the author of *Literacies of Power: What Americans Are Not Allowed to Know* (1994). He collaborated with Paulo Freire on many books and projects, including *Literacy: Reading the Word and the World* (1987) and *Ideology Matters* (forthcoming).